Oxford Picture Dictionary for the Content Areas

Reproducible Collection
Topics 1-22

Social Studies: People and Places

Dorothy Kauffman

198 Madison Avenue
New York, NY 10016 USA

Great Clarendon Street, Oxford OX2 6DP UK

Oxford University Press is a department of the University of Oxford.
It furthers the University's objective of excellence in research, scholarship,
and education by publishing worldwide in

Oxford   New York

Auckland   Cape Town   Dar es Salaam   Hong Kong   Karachi
Kuala Lumpur   Madrid   Melbourne   Mexico City   Nairobi
New Delhi   Shanghai   Taipei   Toronto

With offices in
Argentina   Austria   Brazil   Chile   Czech Republic   France   Greece
Guatemala   Hungary   Italy   Japan   Poland   Portugal   Singapore
South Korea   Switzerland   Thailand   Turkey   Ukraine   Vietnam

OXFORD and OXFORD ENGLISH are registered trademarks of
Oxford University Press.

© Oxford University Press 2010

Database right Oxford University Press (maker)

All rights reserved. No part of this publication may be reproduced,
stored in a retrieval system, or transmitted, in any form or by any means,
without the prior permission in writing of Oxford University Press (with
the sole exception of photocopying carried out under the conditions stated
in the paragraph headed "Photocopying"), or as expressly permitted by law, or
under terms agreed with the appropriate copyright clearance organization.
Enquiries concerning reproduction outside the scope of the above should
be sent to the ELT Rights Department, Oxford University Press, at the
address above.

You must not circulate this book in any other binding or cover
and you must impose this same condition on any acquirer.

Photocopying

The Publisher grants permission for the photocopying of those pages marked
"photocopiable" according to the following conditions. Individual purchasers
may make copies for their own use or for use by classes that they teach.
School purchasers may make copies for use by staff and students, but this
permission does not extend to additional schools or branches.

Under no circumstances may any part of this book be photocopied for resale.

Any websites referred to in this publication are in the public domain and
their addresses are provided by Oxford University Press for information only.
Oxford University Press disclaims any responsibility for the content.

Executive Publishing Manager: Stephanie Karras
Senior Managing Editor: Sharon Sargent
Development Editor: Brandon Lord
Art and Design Director: Susan Sanguily
Senior Production Artist: Julie Armstrong
Cover Design: Sangeeta E. Ramcharan
Senior Image Manager: Trisha Masterson
Design Production Manager: Stephen White
Senior Manufacturing Controller: Eve Wong

Illustrations by: Laurie A. Conley: 78 and 108; Blue Fly Art & Design; and
Mary Chandler.

Cover photo by: K-PHOTOS/Alamy.

ISBN: 978-0-19-452508-4

Printed in China

10 9 8 7 6 5 4 3

This book is printed on paper from certified and well-managed sources.

Table of Contents

Teaching Notes iv

Unit 1 — General Knowledge

1. The Classroom 2
2. The School 7
3. The House 12
4. The Family 17
5. Feelings 22
6. The City 27
7. The Suburbs 32
8. The Country 37
9. The Hospital 42
10. People at Work 47

Unit 2 — The U.S. and the World

11. The United States and U.S. Territories 52
12. The Northeast 61
13. The South 66
14. The Midwest 71
15. The Mountain West 76
16. The Northwest 81
17. The Southwest 86
18. The West Coast and Pacific 91
19. Canada and Mexico 96
20. Europe, Russia, and the Independent Republics 101
21. Asia, Africa, and Australia 106
22. Central and South America and the Caribbean 111

Answer Key 116

Teaching with the *Oxford Picture Dictionary for the Content Areas Reproducible Collection*
by Kate Kinsella and Tonya Ward Singer

The *Reproducible Collection* consists of photocopiable Worksheets and Word and Picture Cards for every *Dictionary* topic. The Worksheets help students learn academic content while developing fluency in reading, while the Word and Picture Cards provide additional vocabulary practice.

Pre-Reading

 **Activity A**

- Prepare to complete the graphic organizer by writing these sentence frames on the board:

    A: This is ____.

    B: That's right. This is ____.
    or
    No. That's not right. This is ____.

- Read the directions chorally and model how to complete the graphic organizer. Point to the picture or blank and then the first sentence frame on the board. Say: *This is a ____ (target word).* Have students chorally repeat. Guide students in writing the correct word in the blank.

- Set up partnering to complete the graphic organizer. Explain that students will use the sentence frames on the board to discuss each picture or blank. Model this process with an additional item. Then chorally read the frames and explain that students will take turns going first.

- Structure the first partner interaction: *Everyone look at the second blank. Think of the word that goes (here/with this picture). Partner 1, tell partner 2, "This is a ____." Now, partner 2, think "Is that right or not?" Answer using the frame.* Point to the written frames.

- Monitor interactions and select one student to share the correct answer. Direct all students to write the answer.

- Repeat this process for the next item with partner 2 beginning the dialog.

- Have students complete any remaining items. Remind them they need to first discuss and agree upon each answer before writing it.

- Monitor responses and re-teach as necessary.

- Conclude the activity by calling on different students to share the answers as you write them for the class to see. Ensure students use the frames to share in a complete sentence.

 **Activity B**

- To build oral language and literacy, students will: (1) read the item silently, (2) think of the best way to complete the sentence, (3) share the answer with a partner, (4) agree on the best answer, and (5) write the answer.

- Read the directions chorally and then model the process with the first item. Provide students with these frames to help them agree upon the best answer:

    A: (Read the sentence to your partner.)

    B: I agree. I think the answer is ____ (read the sentence).
    or
    I disagree. I think the answer is ____ (read the sentence).

- For the next item, indicate which partner will begin. Monitor responses and then choose individuals to report.

- Direct students to continue this process with the remaining items in the activity. Check for understanding, and conclude with student sharing as you write correct answers for students to see.

Activity C

- Explain the partner task. Have students point to the directions and read them chorally with you.

- Read aloud the model dialog and the first sentence frame. Explain what is necessary to complete the task.

- Model the partner process. Pair students. Indicate which partner will share first.

- Monitor student responses and re-teach as needed. If students are successful with the initial item, have them continue completing the sentences with their partner. If students are struggling, model and guide practice.

- After partners interact, call on individuals to share with the whole group.

Page 19 in the *OPD for the Content Areas Reproducible Collection*, Life Science, Activity C

C Work with a partner. Talk about exploring science. Look at page 103 in the *Dictionary*. Use the chart in A. Take turns. Keep going.

A: What is used for measuring?
B: A meter stick is used for measuring.
B: What is used for _____?
A: A _____ is used for _____.

©Oxford University Press 2010. Limited permission granted to photocopy.   19

Read and Connect

- Have students point to the directions and read them chorally with you.

- Introduce the reading: *Today we are going to read about _____.* Point to the title. *Let's read the title together.*

First Read: Model Fluent Reading

- Read the passage out loud using oral cloze. With oral cloze, the teacher reads the text aloud and omits a word every other sentence. Students follow along reading silently and chime in chorally when the teacher omits a word. This process ensures that students focus on decoding the words as they listen to fluent reading with accurate pronunciation, intonation, and pausing.

- Prepare for oral cloze by underlining words to omit. Only omit words that carry meaning, such as nouns and verbs. Don't omit structural words such as *the, of, because,* or the first word in a sentence.

- As you begin reading with oral cloze, tell students: *Now we will read the text together using oral cloze. I'll read the text aloud. Follow along silently and point to the words as I read. When you hear me stop and not say a word, read that word aloud together. Let's practice with the first sentence.... That's right. Now let's read from the beginning again.*

Second Read: Identify Text Structure

- Reread the first paragraph and put a star next to the main idea. Say: *This is the main idea of the reading. The reading is mostly about _____ (main idea). Let's read the topic sentence of each paragraph to see what details we will find in the reading.*

- Have students point to paragraph two. Read the topic sentence, first using oral cloze, then chorally. State simply what the paragraph will be about. Repeat for the remaining paragraphs to give students a quick overview of the text organization.

- Reread the entire text using oral cloze. This time omit different words and pick up the pace slightly.

Third Read: Build Reading Fluency

- Have students read the text a third time using partner cloze. Partner cloze ensures accountable rereading because each student has an active role. One student assumes the teacher role, reading aloud and omitting a word every other sentence. The partner follows along, reading silently, and chimes in when the partner omits a word.

- The first few times you use partner cloze, choose a student to be your partner and model the process. Sit side-by-side close together, speak in low voices, and read at an appropriate pace.

- Prepare students for effective partner cloze by first having them read the text and underline a word in every other sentence to omit. Remind them to select words that have a lot of meaning in the sentence, such as nouns and verbs. Give examples including topic words from the unit. Tell them not underline structural words like *the*, *of*, or *because*.

Fourth Read: Increase Comprehension

 **Activity D**

There are three types of comprehension exercises to the right of the passage: (1) underlining important details, (2) locating information, and (3) identifying the main idea. Focus on one item at a time, using teacher modeling, guided practice, and partner interaction.

- Focus on one exercise at a time. Begin by reading the directions chorally and modeling how to complete the first activity.
- Read the second activity chorally. Have students brainstorm responses with a partner. Monitor responses as students interact and choose individuals to report appropriate answer(s). Guide all students in locating and pointing to the information in the text.
- If students need additional guidance, repeat this process with the next activity. If they are ready for more independence, have them individually complete the remaining items before comparing responses with a partner. Be sure to structure this interaction by first modeling and providing appropriate sentence frames.

Post-Reading

 **Activity E**

- If students are unfamiliar with true and false items, write the words and definitions on the board: *True = correct or right. False = wrong or not right.*
- To model the concepts, write three obvious true statements on the board related to students' shared experiences. For example: *Our classroom is room ____. Our teacher is ____ (your name). Our school is ____ (name of school).* Then rewrite these same statements, supplying false content.

- 👥 Read the directions for the post-reading true and false activity. Model the process of the partner dialog with the content about your classroom. Then have partners practice with this familiar content.
- Explain that students will now follow the same process with statements about the reading. Read the first model and then have students reread the text to find the correct content.
- Guide students in completing the next example with content that is either true or false. Structure the partner interaction.
- If students have trouble coming up with new statements about the text, model how they can find and underline a true detail in the text, and change it slightly to make it a false detail.

 **Organizing Ideas for Writing with a Graphic Organizer**

- Explain that the purpose of the chart is to brainstorm and organize ideas for the writing activity. Read the writing activity instructions and the beginning of the paragraph to help students focus their brainstorming.
- Model adding a few relevant details to the graphic organizer and articulating the ideas in a complete sentence. Explain that students will work with a partner to first brainstorm and then write their ideas.
- Provide relevant response frame(s) to bolster language production during partner interactions For example, for Activity F on page 103 (in *Social Studies: People and Places*): *One country in (Western/Central/Eastern) Europe is ____.* When possible, use the frames from the paragraph to directly prepare students for the writing activity.

Page 103 in the *OPD for the Content Areas Reproducible Collection, Social Studies: People and Places*, Activities F–G

F Make a chart about some regions and countries of Europe.

Regions of Europe

Western Europe	Central Europe	Eastern Europe

G Use the chart in F. Write about Europe.

Regions of Europe

There are many regions and countries in Europe. One country in Western Europe is _____. Another is _____. Two countries in Central Europe are _____.

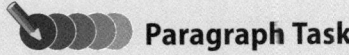 **Paragraph Task**

- Read the directions chorally and introduce the activity. Say: *Now we're going to write a paragraph about (this picture/your graphic organizer) using the language we've learned to talk about ___ (the topic). Part of the paragraph is already written for us. Let's read the title and topic sentence to see what the paragraph is mainly about.*

- Project the paragraph frame with an overhead projector. Read the title and topic sentence chorally with students. Circle key words in the topic sentence.

- Guide students in studying the picture or reviewing their graphic organizer to identify details that support the paragraph topic. Have partners articulate what they see in the picture or what they put in the graphic organizer. Provide sentence frames to coach students in using complete sentences. For example, for Activity F on page 21 (in *Life Science*): *One step I see is ___.* Call on volunteers to share one idea out loud. Write their ideas on the board.

- Reread the topic sentence. Then ask for suggestions to complete the first sentence frame. Read the completed sentence as the first supporting detail and show how it supports the main idea.

- Guide the students to complete the second supporting detail. Read the sentence frame out loud and then have students brainstorm responses with a partner. Monitor interactions and choose individuals to report appropriate answer(s). Model completing the sentence frame in the projected paragraph, and have students fill in the appropriate information.

- In the remaining blank lines, direct students to write two sentences on their own. Encourage them to use the same sentence pattern as the provided frames.

Differentiation Note

●●● For these students, write possible answers to the sentence frames on the board and guide partner practice to ensure success.

- After students complete their paragraphs, have them edit their work for the following: (1) beginning sentences with a capital letter, (2) ending sentences with a period, and (3) spelling topic terms correctly.

Differentiation Note

●●● Have these students add one or two more sentences to the projected paragraph. Ask these students to read aloud their contributed sentences.

- Finally, have students read their completed paragraph to a partner.

Using the Word and Picture Cards

- The Word and Picture Cards are useful for re-teaching and review. As you prepare these resources, you may choose to copy the pictures and terms on separate pages for matching activities, or copy them aligned back-to-back to create two-sided flashcards.

- There are many ways to use the Picture Cards for independent, partner, or small-group review. Popular activities include matching the terms to pictures, memory games, or review with flashcards. To both review content and maximize oral language output, provide sentence frames and structure student dialogs during each activity.

- For example, try this variation of Bingo to maximize oral language production. Have each student choose three picture cards. Put the word cards in a bag and select one at a time to read as you would in a bingo game. For each term, ask: *Do you have the ___?* Have students chorally repeat: *Yes, I have the ___.* or, *No, I don't have the ___.* When a student's picture is called, they turn it face down. When all three pictures are face down, they shout *bingo!* Students then pick three new pictures to repeat the game.

Reproducible Collection   Teaching Notes

TOPIC 1

The Classroom

Pre-reading

A Complete the idea web. What is in the classroom?

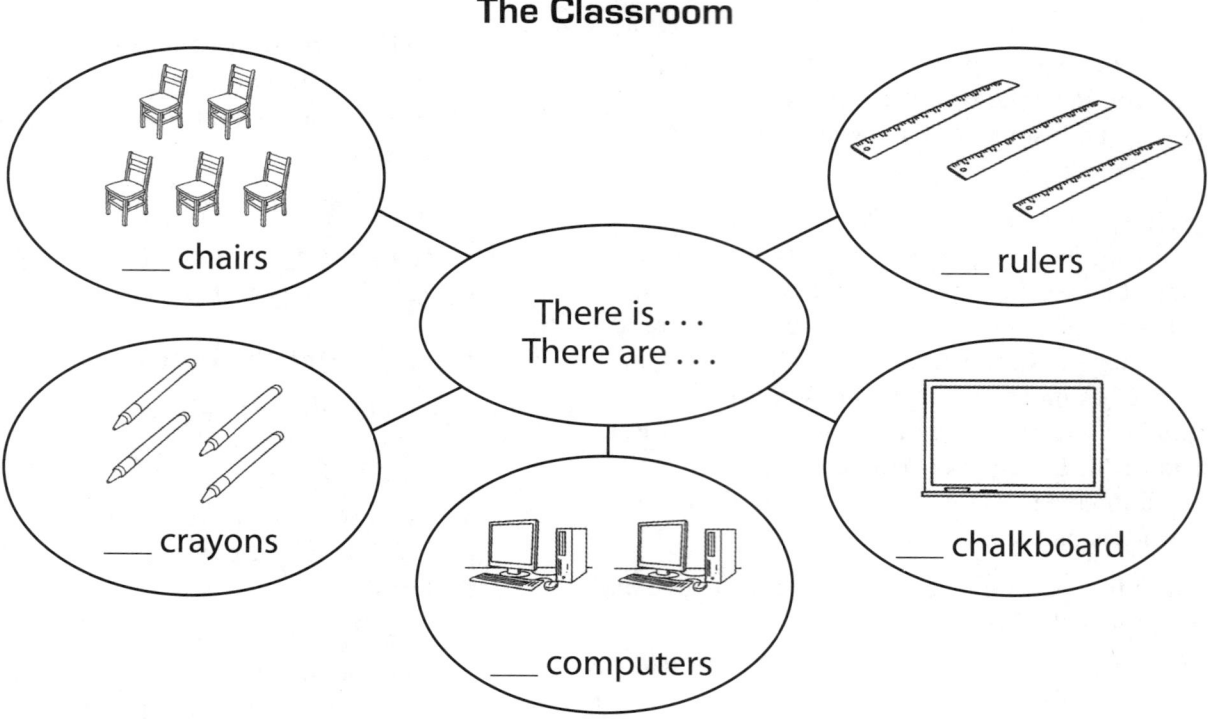

B Look at the idea web in A. Complete the sentences.

1. There are _____ computers.
2. There are _____ chairs.
3. There is _____ chalkboard.
4. There are _____ crayons.

C Work with a partner. Talk about the classroom. Look at page 3 in the *Dictionary*. Use the idea web in A. Take turns. Keep going.

A: Are there four computers in the classroom?

B: No, there are two computers in the classroom.

B: How many _____ are there in the classroom?

A: There are _____ in the classroom.

The Classroom
Read and Connect

D Read about the people and things in the classroom.

The Classroom

1   My name is Anita. This is my classroom. There are people and many useful things in my classroom.

2   We have one teacher. Her name is Mrs. Salinas. There are ten students in the classroom. There are seven girls and there are three boys. Five students are sitting in chairs and four students work on the floor. One student is at the computer. Can you find me? I am at the pencil sharpener.

3   There are many things in the classroom, too. There is one whiteboard. There is a map on the whiteboard. There is one bulletin board. We keep a calendar on the bulletin board. There is a chalkboard in the classroom, too.

4   There are two tables in the classroom. A computer is on one of the tables, and another computer is on a desk. There are chairs in the classroom. There is a flag in the classroom. There is a clock on the wall. The students on the floor use crayons, paper, and a ruler. A notebook, a pencil, and a pen are also on the floor. A pair of scissors and a bottle of glue are on the floor, too.

5   How many people are in your classroom? What things are in your classroom?

---

1. **Read the questions. Find and underline the answers in the reading.**
   a. How many students are in the classroom?
   b. How many computers are in the classroom?
   c. How many clocks are on the wall?
   d. How many flags are in the classroom?

2. **Complete the sentences.**
   a. The information about scissors and glue is in paragraph ___.
   b. The information about the bulletin board is in paragraph ___.
   c. The information about the calendar is in paragraph ___.

3. **What is the main idea?**
   a. The main idea is in paragraph ___.
   b. The main idea is _____

Name _____

The Classroom
Post-reading

E Work with a partner. Partner A: Say a sentence about the reading in D. Partner B: Is the sentence *true* or *false*? Make false sentences true. Take turns. Keep going.

A: There are two clocks in the classroom.

B: False. There is _____.

B: There are _____.

A: _____

A: _____

B: _____

F Make an idea web about the people and things in your classroom.

My Classroom

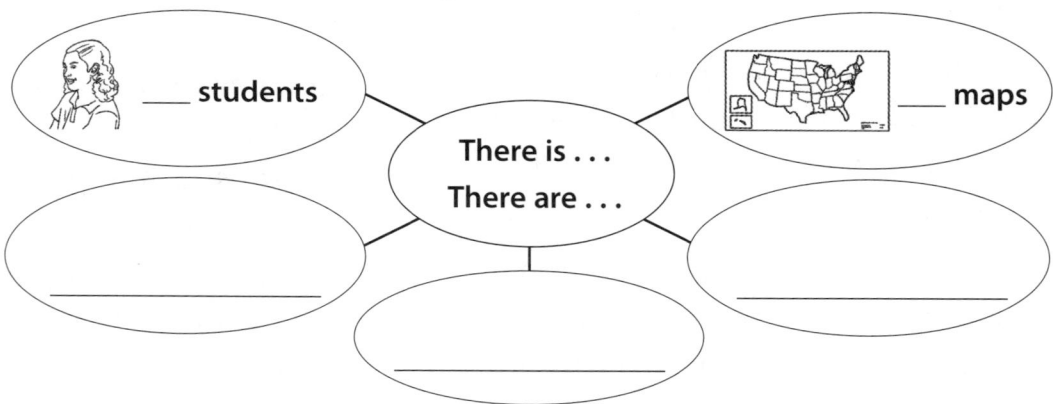

G Use the idea web in F. Write about your classroom.

My Classroom

There are many people and things in my classroom. There are _____ students. There are _____ girls and there are _____.

_____

_____

_____

4   ©Oxford University Press 2010. Limited permission granted to photocopy.

Topic 1 Word and Picture Cards

computer	bulletin board	map	whiteboard
pencil sharpener	chalkboard	chair	table
student	pen	pencil	desk
ruler	book	paper	teacher
wastebasket	notebook	glue	crayon

Topic 1 Word and Picture Cards

TOPIC 2

The School
Pre-reading

A Complete the chart. Where do people work?

People and Places in School

B Look at the chart in A. Complete the sentences.

1. The coach works in the _____.
2. The _____ works in the library.
3. The custodian works in the _____.
4. The _____ works in the office.

C Work with a partner. Talk about people and places in school. Look at page 5 in the *Dictionary*. Use the chart in A. Take turns. Keep going.

A: Where does the coach work?

B: The coach works in the gym.

B: Where does the _____ work?

A: The _____ works in the _____.

The School
Read and Connect

D Read about people and places in school.

People and Places in School

1   This is Marco's first day of school. There are many different rooms and many people in his new school.

2   Marco sees many important rooms on the first floor. The office is on the first floor. The principal works in the office. The principal is in charge of the school. The secretary works near the principal's office. The cafeteria is on the first floor, too. The students eat lunch in the cafeteria. The gym is also on the first floor. The coach is in the gym. Students play basketball in the gym.

3   On the second floor, Marco sees more new rooms and people. The hall is on the second floor. The water fountain is in the hall. The girls room and the boys room are in the hall, too. There are lockers in the hall. The custodian is in the hall. The custodian cleans the school. The auditorium is also on the second floor. There is a concert in the auditorium.

4   Marco's new school has a third floor, too. He walks up the stairs to the library. Students read in the library. The librarian helps the students. The media center is in the library. Students watch videos in the media center.

5   Marco likes his new school. He likes all the new rooms and people, too. Marco is happy to be at school.

---

1. Read the questions. Find and <u>underline</u> the answers in the reading.
   a. Who eats lunch in the cafeteria?
   b. Where is the water fountain?
   c. Who helps students in the library?
   d. Where is the media center?

2. Complete the sentences.
   a. The information about the custodian is in paragraph ___.
   b. The information about the library is in paragraph ___.
   c. The information about the office is in paragraph ___.

3. What is the main idea?
   a. The main idea is in paragraph ___.
   b. The main idea is _____
   _____
   _____

TOPIC 2: The School
Post-reading

E Work with a partner. Partner A: Say a sentence about the reading in D. Partner B: Is the sentence *true* or *false*? Make false sentences true. Take turns. Keep going.

A: The custodian works in the library.

B: False. The custodian works in the _____.

B: The coach works _____.

A: _____

A: _____

B: _____

F Make a People and Places chart about your school.

People and Places in My School

People				
Places				

G Use the chart in F. Write about your school.

People and Places in My School

There are many different rooms and many people at my school.

The _____ is on the _____ floor of the school.

The _____ works in the _____.

_____

_____

_____

Topic 2 Word and Picture Cards

playground	office	principal	secretary
cafeteria	gym	coach	hall
water fountain	locker	boys room	girls room
custodian	auditorium	stairs	library
librarian	media center		

Topic 2 Word and Picture Cards

TOPIC 3

The House

Pre-reading

A Complete the chart. Use the words in the box. Where are the rooms in the house? What is in each room?

> attic   kitchen   basement   sink

Rooms in the House

	Bathroom	Bedroom	Kitchen	Living Room
Above it	attic	_____	bathroom	bedroom
Below it	kitchen	living room	_____	basement
Next to it	bedroom	bathroom	living room	_____
In it	_____	closet	cupboard	floor

B Look at the chart in A. Complete the sentences.

1. The living room is above the _____.
2. The _____ is next to the bathroom.
3. The cupboard is in the _____.
4. The _____ is below the bedroom.

C Work with a partner. Talk about the picture of the house. Look at page 7 in the *Dictionary*. Use the chart in A. Take turns. Keep going.

A: Which room is above the bedroom?

B: The attic is above the bedroom.

B: Which room is below the _____?

A: The _____ is below the _____.

TOPIC 3: The House
Read and Connect

D Read about the rooms and things in the house.

The Gilmans' House

1. The Gilman family has a big yellow house. There are many rooms and useful things in the Gilmans' house. There is a roof above the house and the porch. A chimney is at one end of the roof. The attic is the top floor of the house. The family stores things in the attic.

2. The bathroom and bedroom are below the attic. Sam is in the bathroom. He is washing his face at the sink. The sink is next to the toilet and the bathtub. The bedroom is next to the bathroom. Janet is sleeping in the bedroom. There are pictures on the wall above the bed. The closet door is open. There is a light on the ceiling.

3. The kitchen is next to the living room. It is on the first floor. Mrs. Gilman and Tanya are in the kitchen. Mrs. Gilman is eating breakfast. Tanya is getting a plate from the cupboard. Alex and Troy are watching TV in the living room. Troy is standing on the rug on the floor. They are ready for school.

4. Mr. Gilman is in the basement. He is doing laundry. The basement is below the living room and the kitchen.

5. Pete is on the front porch. He is leaving early for school.

---

1. **Read the questions. Find and <u>underline</u> the answers in the reading.**
   a. Where is the basement?
   b. What is the sink next to?
   c. Where are Mrs. Gilman and Tanya?
   d. What is Pete doing?

2. **Complete the sentences.**
   a. The information about the roof is in paragraph ___.
   b. The information about the bedroom is in paragraph ___.
   c. The information about Mr. Gilman is in paragraph ___.
   d. The information about the attic is in paragraph ___.

3. **What is the main idea?**
   a. The main idea is in paragraph ___.
   b. The main idea is _____
   _____
   _____

The House
Post-reading

E Work with a partner. Partner A: Say a sentence about the reading in D. Partner B: Is the sentence *true* or *false*? Make false sentences true. Take turns. Keep going.

A: Mr. Gilman is washing laundry.

B: True. Mr. Gilman is washing laundry.

B: Tanya is in the living room.

A: False. Tanya is in _____.

A: _____

B: _____

F Make a chart about the rooms and things in your home.

Rooms in My Home

	Kitchen	Living Room	Bedroom
Above it			
Below it			
Next to it			
In it			

G Use the chart in F. Write about your home.

Rooms in My Home

There are different rooms in my home. In my home, there is a _____. It is next to the _____. There is a _____ in the kitchen. There is a _____. _____

_____

_____

Topic 3 Word and Picture Cards

porch	window	door	basement
kitchen	cupboard	living room	floor
bathroom	toilet	sink	bathtub
shower	bedroom	closet	wall
ceiling	attic	roof	chimney

Topic 3 Word and Picture Cards

TOPIC 4

The Family

Pre-reading

A Complete the family tree. How are people in the family related to each other?

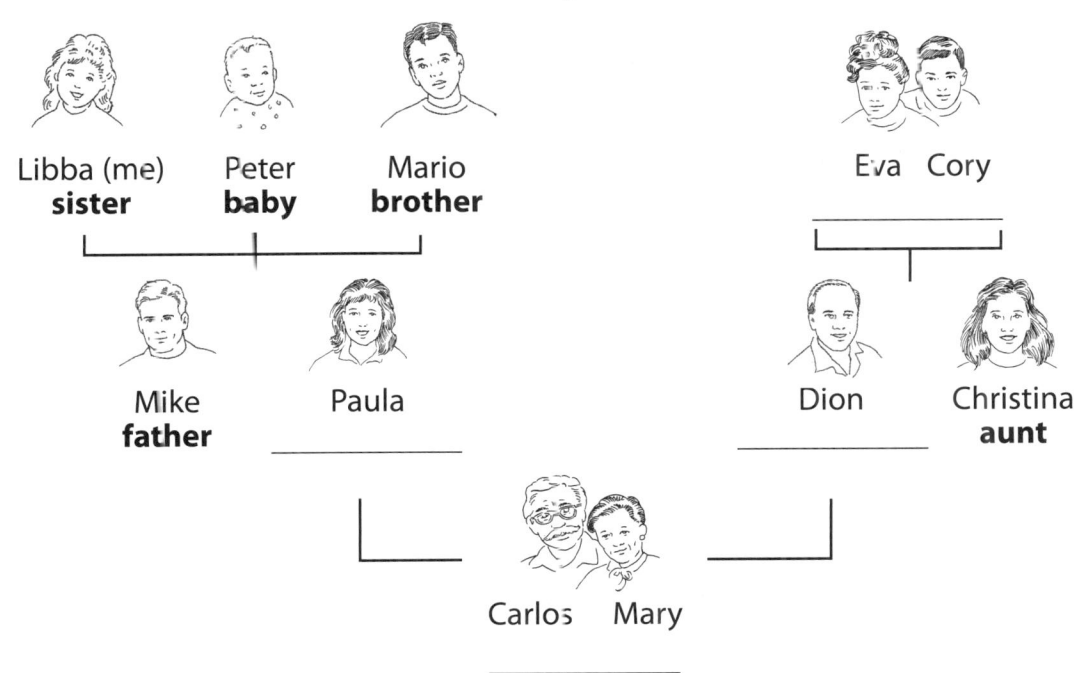

B Use the family tree in A. Complete the sentences.

1. Paula is Peter's _____.
2. Mike is Mario's _____.
3. Libba's brothers are _____ and Peter.
4. Cory and _____ are Libba's cousins.

C Work with a partner. Talk about the family. Look at page 9 in the *Dictionary*. Use the family tree in A. Take turns. Keep going.

A: Who are Libba's parents?
B: Paula and Mike are Libba's parents.
B: Who are Libba's grandparents?
A: Mary and _____ are Libba's grandparents.

©Oxford University Press 2010. Limited permission granted to photocopy.

The Family
Read and Connect

D Read about the people in the family.

Libba's Family

1   My name is Libba Ramos. This is my family. We are having a picnic. The diagram is our family tree. It shows how the people in our family are related.

2   My grandparents are at the bottom of the family tree. Carlos is my grandfather. Mary is my grandmother. Carlos and Mary have two children. Paula is their daughter. Dion is their son. Paula and Dion are brother and sister.

3   Paula is married to Mike. They are my parents. Paula is my mother and Mike is my father. They have three children. I am the oldest of their children. I have two brothers named Mario and Peter. Peter is a baby. He is the youngest. I am Peter and Mario's sister.

4   Dion is our uncle. Dion is married to Christina. Christina is our aunt. They are parents, too. Dion and Christina have two children. Their children are Cory and Eva. Cory and Eva are cousins to me, Mario, and Peter.

5   At the picnic, my grandfather is reading to me and my mother. My grandmother is playing with my brother, Peter. My aunt is getting food out. My uncle and cousins are playing. Our family picnic is fun.

1. **Read the questions. Find and <u>underline</u> the answers in the reading.**
   a. Who is Libba's grandmother?
   b. What are the names of Christina's children?
   c. Who is Peter's sister?
   d. Who is Libba's grandfather?

2. **Complete the sentences.**
   a. The information about Mario and Peter is in paragraph ___.
   b. The information about what a family tree shows is in paragraph ___.
   c. The information about Dion's children is in paragraph ___.
   d. The information about the picnic is in paragraph ___.

3. **What is the main idea?**
   a. The main idea is in paragraph ___.
   b. The main idea is _____

The Family

Post-reading

E Work with a partner. Partner A: Say a sentence about the reading in D. Partner B: Is the sentence *true* or *false*? Make false sentences true. Take turns. Keep going.

A: Cory and Mario are brothers.

B: False. Cory and Mario are _____.

B: Christina is _____'s mother.

A: _____

A: _____

B: _____

F Make a family tree for your family.

My Family Tree

G Use your family tree. Write about people in your family.

My Family

This is my family. My name is _____. My grandfather's name is _____. My grandmother's name is _____.

_____

_____

Topic 4 Word and Picture Cards

grandparents	grandmother	grandfather	parents
mother	father	baby	sister
brother	aunt	uncle	cousins

Topic 4 Word and Picture Cards

TOPIC 5

Feelings

Pre-reading

A Complete the idea web. How do the people feel?

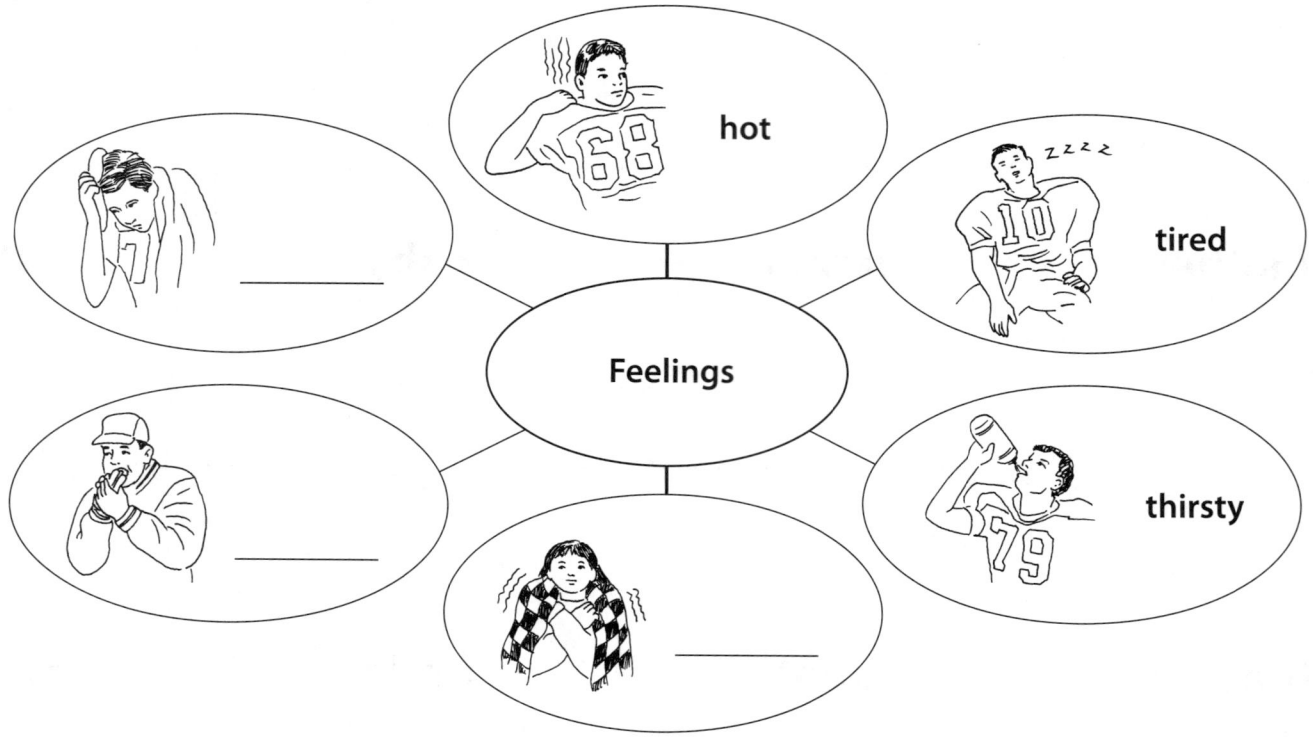

B Look at the idea web in A. Complete the sentences.

1. Number 68 feels _____.
2. Number 10 is _____.
3. The man with a sandwich is _____.
4. Number 7 feels _____.

C Work with a partner. Talk about feelings. Look at page 11 in the *Dictionary*. Use the idea web in A. Take turns. Keep going.

A: Number 78 is thirsty, isn't he?

B: Yes, he is thirsty.

B: The girl with the blanket feels _____, doesn't she?

A: No, she doesn't. She is _____.

Feelings
Read and Connect

D Read about how people feel at a football game.

Feelings at the Football Game

1   People have many kinds of feelings. Physical feelings are the ways our bodies feel. For example, we feel our stomachs rumble when we are hungry. Emotional feelings are how we feel about people and events. For example, we feel happy when our favorite teams win games.

2   Many people are at a football game. Some people are happy. Their team is playing well. The cheerleader is excited about the game. One girl feels cold, so she puts a blanket around her shoulders. The girl's father is hungry, so he eats a sandwich.

3   Some players sit on the bench. Number 7 feels sick. His head hurts. Number 10 is very tired from running. Number 78 is thirsty, so he drinks water. Number 68 is really hot. He pulls on his shirt to let cool air in. Number 33 and another player are angry with each other.

4   The players in red win the game! Later they have a parade. There are clowns at the parade. One clown squirts water at a boy. The boy is surprised. His sister is scared. She does not like the clowns.

5   Everyone celebrates on the street. Number 79 feels proud. He likes to win football games.

1. **Read the questions. Find and underline the answers in the reading.**
   a. Who feels hungry?
   b. Who is excited?
   c. How does Number 79 feel?
   d. What are physical feelings?

2. **Complete the sentences.**
   a. The information about who is tired is in paragraph ___.
   b. The information about emotional feelings is in paragraph ___.
   c. The information about how Number 68 feels is in paragraph ___.
   d. The information about the clowns is in paragraph ___.

3. **What is the main idea?**
   a. The main idea is in paragraph ___.
   b. The main idea is _____
   _____
   _____

Name _____

Feelings
Post-reading

E Work with a partner. Partner A: Say a sentence about the reading in D. Partner B: Is the sentence *true* or *false*? Make false sentences true. Take turns. Keep going.

A: Number 33 is tired.

B: False. Number 33 is _____.

B: Number 68 _____.

A: _____

F Make an idea web about feelings. Write about how your classmates feel on Fridays.

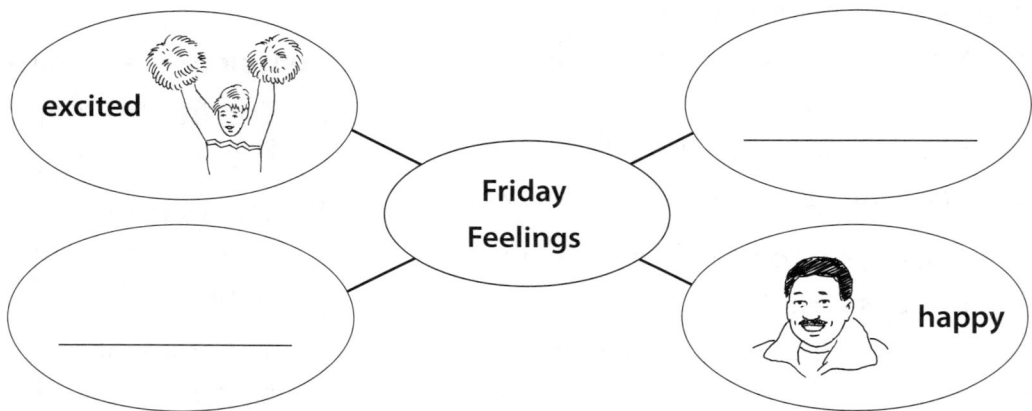

G Use the idea web in F. Write about how you and your classmates feel on Fridays.

Friday Feelings

On Fridays my classmates have different feelings. In the morning, some students feel _____. Before lunch, _____

_____

_____

_____

Topic 5 Word and Picture Cards

hot	thirsty	tired	sick
shy	silly	hungry	cold
sad	proud	surprised	scared
angry	excited	lonely	happy

Topic 5 Word and Picture Cards

TOPIC 6

The City

Pre-reading

A Complete the chart. Where are some things and places in the city?

Things and Places

Place or Thing		Place
The bank is	behind	the movie theater
The post office is	between	the department store and the _____
The _____ is	across the street from	the restaurant

B Look at the chart in A. Complete the sentences.

1. The bank is _____ the movie theater.
2. The post office is _____ the department store and the hotel.
3. The bus is across the street from the _____.
4. The restaurant is across the street from _____.

C Work with a partner. Talk about places in the city. Look at page 13 in the *Dictionary*. Use the chart in A. Take turns. Keep going.

A: Where is the newsstand?

B: The newsstand is close to the restaurant.

B: What is behind the department store?

A: The _____ is behind the department store.

The City
Read and Connect

D Read about things and places in the city.

The City

1   There are many people and many buildings in a city. Do you know where one building is located? You can use this knowledge to describe other places.

2   In this city, a subway entrance is close to the police station. People use the subway to travel under the city. Many people walk a lot. They ride in cars, taxis, and buses, too. Some even fly above the city in helicopters!

3   An office building is across the street from the subway. A restaurant is on the first floor of the office building. There is a newsstand close to the office building. People buy newspapers at the newsstand.

4   The hotel is between the office building and the post office. There is a mailbox in front of the post office. The department store is close to the post office. People buy clothes at the department store.

5   A mosque is behind the department store. There is a temple across the street from the department store. There is a church between the department store and the apartment building. The apartment building is far from the movie theater.

6   Think about a building you know. What is it next to? What is it far from?

1. **Read the questions. Find and <u>underline</u> the answers in the reading.**
   a. Where is the restaurant?
   b. Where is the temple?
   c. What is in front of the post office?
   d. What building is across the street from the subway?

2. **Complete the sentences.**
   a. The information about how people travel in the city is in paragraph ___.
   b. The information about the apartment building is in paragraph ___.
   c. The information about the police station is in paragraph ___.

3. **What is the main idea?**
   a. The main idea is in paragraph ___.
   b. The main idea is _____
   _____
   _____

The City
Post-reading

E Work with a partner. Partner A: Say a sentence about the reading in D. Partner B: Is the sentence *true* or *false*? Make false sentences true. Take turns. Keep going.

A: The movie theater is _____ the hotel.

B: True. It is _____ the hotel.

B: Many people live in an _____.

A: _____

A: _____

B: _____

F Make a Things and Places chart. Describe where things and places are in your town or city.

Things and Places Where I Live

Place or Thing	🔗	Place

G Use the chart in F. Write about places around you.

Things and Places Where I Live

There are buildings where I live. There is a _____. It is close to _____. There is a _____, too. It is _____

_____

_____

_____

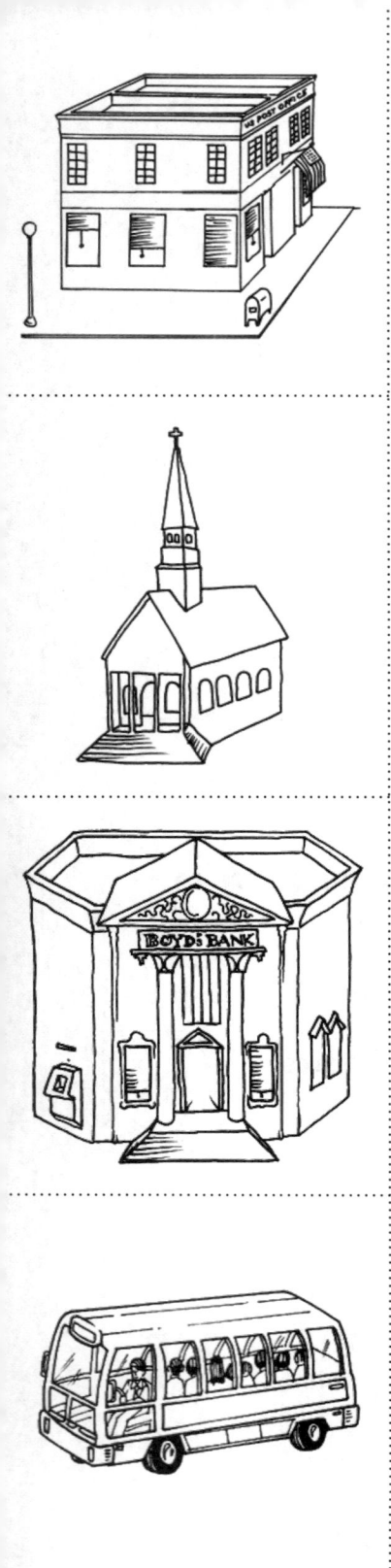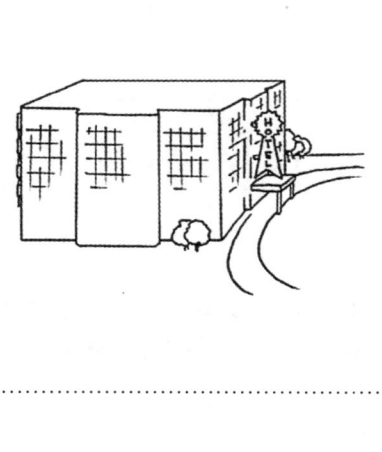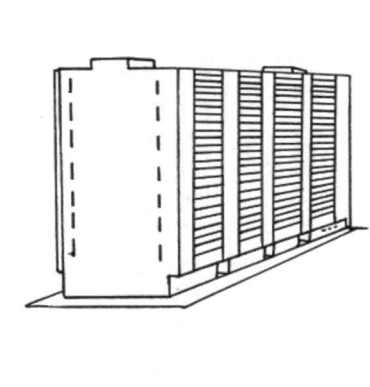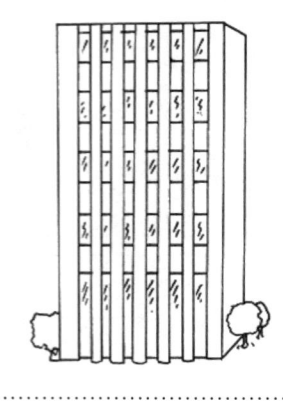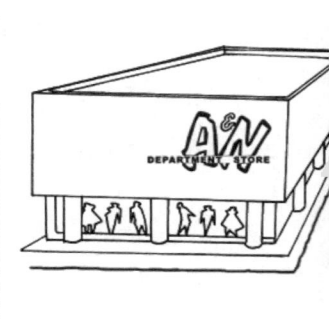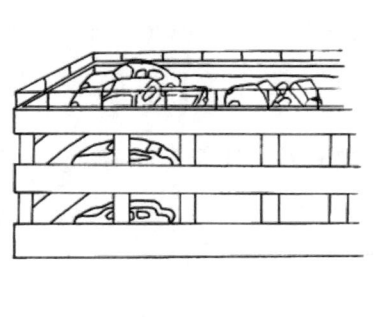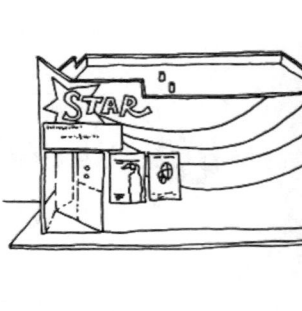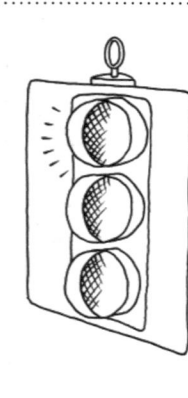

Topic 6 Word and Picture Cards

restaurant	newsstand	hotel	post office
department store	office building	apartment building	church
mosque	temple	parking garage	bank
movie theater	police station	subway	bus
taxi	garbage truck	helicopter	traffic light

TOPIC 7

The Suburbs

Pre-reading

A Complete the chart. Use the words in the box. What things are in the suburbs?

> pool   gas   bicycle

In the Suburbs

Fun Activities	Buildings	Getting Around
grow yellow flowers	a closed garage	an old _____
play at the big park	a new _____ station	a blue car
play a fun game of basketball		a red motorcycle
swim in the swimming _____		a useful van

B Look at the chart in A. Complete the sentences.

1. People can play at the big _____.
2. A _____ station is a building in the suburbs.
3. A blue _____ is a way to get around.
4. People can play a fun game of _____.

C Work with a partner. Talk about the suburbs. Look at page 15 in the *Dictionary*. Use the chart in A. Take turns. Keep going.

A: Is he washing the blue car?
B: Yes, he is.
B: Where are the boys playing basketball?
A: They are playing in a _____.

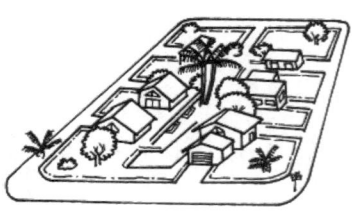

The Suburbs

Read and Connect

D Read about the suburbs.

A Day in the Suburbs

1 Suburbs are outside the main part of a city. In this suburb, there are big houses with green yards and tall trees. Some of the houses have green gardens with vegetables and yellow flowers. There are clean streets and friendly people.

2 People do many things in this suburb. Some people walk on the sidewalk. They cross the street at the white crosswalk. On the corner is a red fire hydrant and a stop sign.

3 People are doing some fun things. Mr. Morse is riding his motorcycle. Troy and Brian are playing basketball. A bicycle is laying on the sidewalk. Some people are playing baseball in the big park. Other people are swimming in the swimming pool.

4 Some people are doing other things. Mr. and Mrs. Hong are taking a long walk around the neighborhood. Mr. Clark is mailing a letter. He is putting it in the blue mailbox. Mr. Addison is washing his car. Mrs. Lopez is buying gas for her van at the new gas station.

5 Do you live in the suburbs? What is your neighborhood like?

1. **Read the questions. Find and <u>underline</u> the answers in the reading.**
   a. What do some houses have?
   b. Who is taking a walk?
   c. What are Troy and Brian doing?
   d. Who is mailing a letter?

2. **Complete the sentences.**
   a. The information about the swimming pool is in paragraph ___.
   b. The information about what Mrs. Lopez is doing is in paragraph ___.
   c. The information about the crosswalk is in paragraph ___.
   d. The information about the gardens is in paragraph ___.

3. **What is the main idea?**
   a. The main idea is in paragraph ___.
   b. The main idea is _____
   _____
   _____

Name _____

The Suburbs
Post-reading

E Work with a partner. Partner A: Say a sentence about the reading in D. Partner B: Is the sentence *true* or *false*? Make false sentences true. Take turns. Keep going.

A: Mr. Addison is washing his house.

B: False. He is washing his _____.

B: Some people in the suburbs have gardens.

A: _____

A: _____

B: _____

F Look at the picture. Complete the paragraph.

A Summer Evening in the Suburbs

The Williams family lives in the suburbs. They were at the neighborhood swimming _____. Jory stops at a _____. He is tying his shoe.

_____

_____

_____

34 ©Oxford University Press 2010. Limited permission granted to photocopy.

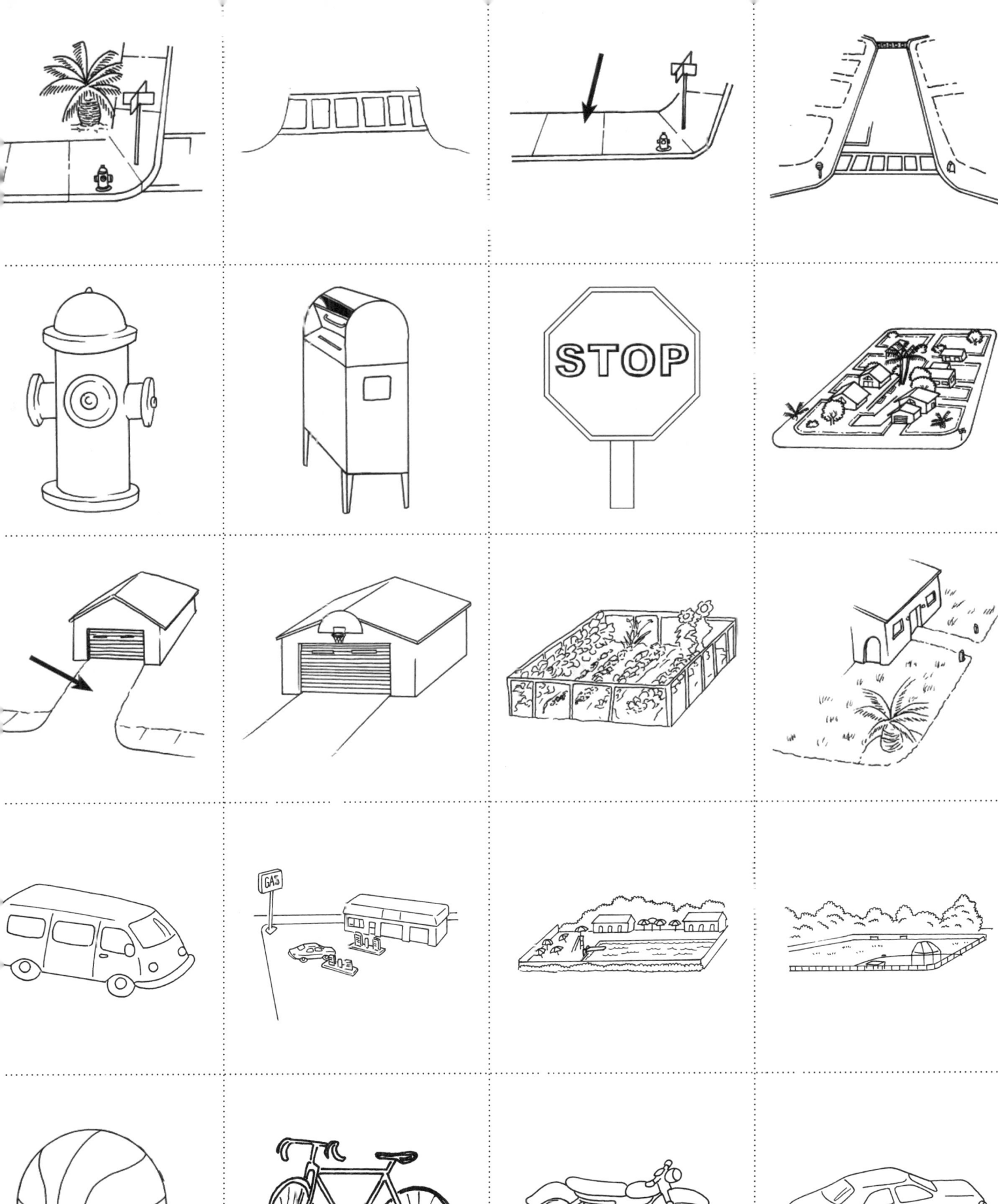

Topic 7 Word and Picture Cards

street	sidewalk	crosswalk	corner
block	stop sign	mailbox	fire hydrant
yard	garden	garage	driveway
park	swimming pool	gas station	van
car	motorcycle	bicycle	basketball

TOPIC 8

The Country

Pre-reading

A Complete the chart. Use the words in the box. What can you find in the country?

> orchard   fence   tractor   inside

Things in the Country

Place or Thing		Place or Thing
There is a _____	around	the pasture.
Some chickens are	_____	the chicken coop.
There is a pond	next to	the _____.
The _____ is	outside	the barn.

B Look at the chart in A. Complete the sentences.

1. Some chickens are inside the chicken _____.
2. The pond is _____ the orchard.
3. There is a fence around the _____.
4. The _____ is outside the barn.

C Work with a partner. Talk about places in the country. Look at page 17 in the *Dictionary*. Use the chart in A. Take turns. Keep going.

A: Where are the sheep?

B: They are _____ the fence.

B: Where are the barn and the house?

A: They are _____ each other.

The Country

Read and Connect

D Read about a farm in the country.

Out in the Country

1   The Garza family has a farm in the country. They have a yellow house. There is a path from the house to the red barn. There is a chicken coop next to the barn. There is a fence around the chicken coop. There is a silo behind the barn. The silo holds grain.

2   The Garzas have a big farm. There are many fields around the house. There is an orchard across the road from the house. Green woods and some hills are behind the orchard. A pasture with a pond is next to the orchard.

3   Many animals live on the farm. There is a horse inside the barn. Two black and white cows are outside the barn. Some chickens are inside the chicken coop. Some white sheep are in the pasture.

4   Everybody on the farm is busy. Mrs. Garza is feeding the chickens. Mr. Garza is driving a tractor. Two children are riding inside the wagon. A neighbor is driving a truck across the bridge. Marco Garza is picking apples in the orchard.

5   The Garzas like their farm. They have lots of fun when they work.

1. **Read the questions. Find and <u>underline</u> the answers in the reading.**
   a. Where is the Garzas' farm?
   b. Where are the fields?
   c. Where are the chickens?
   d. What are the children doing?

2. **Complete the sentences.**
   a. The information about the house is in paragraph ___.
   b. The information about the orchard is in paragraph ___.
   c. The information about the silo is in paragraph ___.
   d. The information about the bridge is in paragraph ___.

3. **What is the main idea?**
   a. The main idea is in paragraph ___.
   b. The main idea is _____
   _____
   _____

TOPIC 8

The Country
Post-reading

E Work with a partner. Partner A: Say a sentence about the reading in D. Partner B: Is the sentence *true* or *false*? Make false sentences true. Take turns. Keep going.

A: Very few animals live on the farm.

B: False. Many animals live on the farm.

B: Mrs. Garza is feeding _____.

A: _____

A: _____

B: _____

F Look at the picture. Complete the paragraph.

The Digmans' Farm

This is the Digman family's farm. A horse is _____ the fence.

There are cows _____ the fence. An orchard is next to the _____.

_____

_____

Topic 8 Word and Picture Cards

farm	barn	silo	path
fence	chicken coop	orchard	pasture
pond	woods	hills	field
road	stream	bridge	airplane
train	truck	tractor	wagon

Topic 8 Word and Picture Cards

TOPIC 9

The Hospital

Pre-reading

A Complete the idea web. Use the words in the box. What things do different people use in a hospital?

> thermometer   crutches   patient

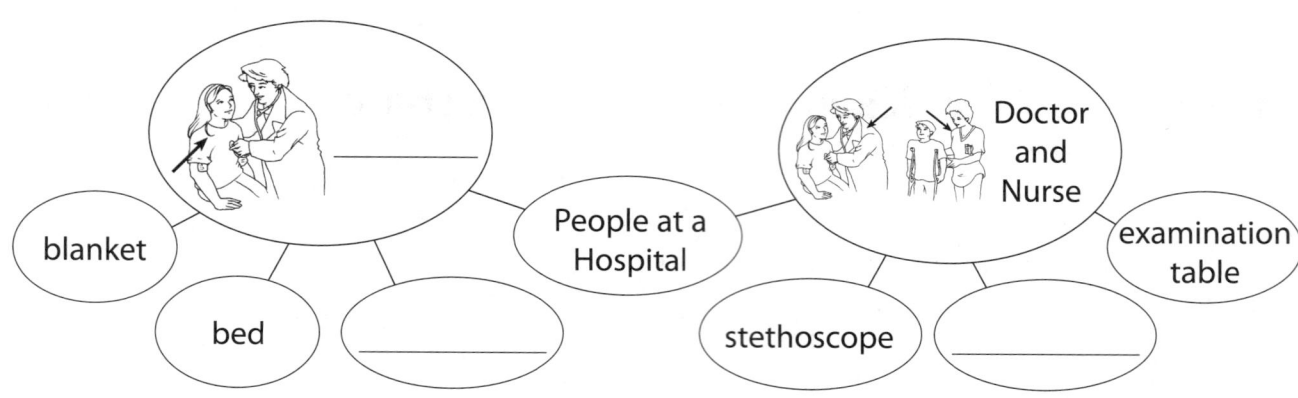

B Look at the idea web in A. Complete the sentences.

1. A _____ needs a blanket.
2. A _____ uses a stethoscope.
3. A _____ sometimes needs crutches.
4. A nurse uses a _____ to take temperatures.

C Work with a partner. Talk about the things in a hospital. Look at page 19 in the *Dictionary*. Use the idea web in A. Take turns. Keep going.

A: Where is the ambulance?
B: The ambulance is outside the hospital.
B: What does the patient lie on?
A: The patient lies on a _____.

TOPIC 9
The Hospital
Read and Connect

D Read about what people are doing in a hospital.

The Hospital

1   People go to a hospital when they are hurt or sick. They need help from doctors and nurses. The hospital is a busy place.

2   A doctor and a patient are in an examination room. The patient is sitting on an examination table. Her arm has a bandage on it. The doctor is using a stethoscope. She is listening to the patient's heart. The doctor is waiting to see the patient's X-ray.

3   One large hospital room has three patients in it. One patient has a broken leg. His leg is in a cast. The nurse is helping him walk with crutches. Another patient is lying in a bed. She is using a blanket. A wheelchair is next to her bed. There is a boy in another bed. He is resting his head on a pillow.

4   There is a new baby in another room. The baby's parents are waiting to take the baby home tomorrow. They are happy.

5   Paramedics use ambulances to bring people to hospitals. They help patients, too. An ambulance is outside the emergency entrance. A paramedic is bringing a patient inside on a stretcher. Nurses and doctors help this patient, too.

6   The doctors and nurses like to help patients in the hospital. They like to make people feel better.

1. **Read the questions. Find and <u>underline</u> the answers in the reading.**
   a. Who is in the examination room?
   b. What can the baby's parents do tomorrow?
   c. What do paramedics do?
   d. How many patients are in the large hospital room?

2. **Complete the sentences.**
   a. The information about the stethoscope is in paragraph ___.
   b. The information about the nurse is in paragraph ___.
   c. The information about the boy with crutches is in paragraph ___.
   d. The information about the new baby is in paragraph ___.

3. **What is the main idea?**
   a. The main idea is in paragraph ___.
   b. The main idea is _____
   _____
   _____

Name _____

The Hospital
Post-reading

E Work with a partner. Partner A: Say a sentence about the reading in D. Partner B: Is the sentence *true* or *false*? Make false sentences true. Take turns. Keep going.

A: A patient is lying in the bed.

B: _____. A patient is lying in the bed.

B: The paramedic is _____.

A: _____

A: _____

B: _____

F Look at the picture. Complete the paragraph.

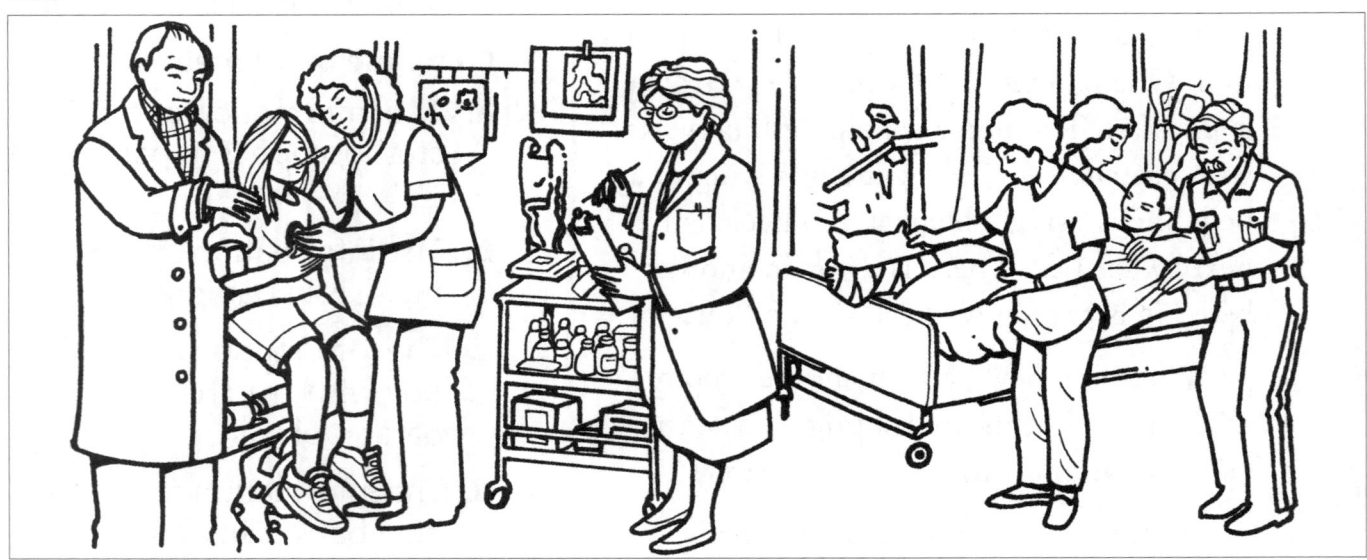

In the Hospital

Tonight is a busy night at the hospital. In one room, a _____ tells the

_____ how she feels. The nurse is using a _____. The doctor

_____

_____

_____

Topic 9 Word and Picture Cards

patient	doctor	examination table	bandage
stethoscope	thermometer	medicine	X-ray
nurse	crutches	cast	wheelchair
bed	pillow	blanket	ambulance
paramedic	stretcher		

TOPIC 10

People at Work

Pre-reading

A Complete the chart. What jobs do people do?

People at Work

Worker	What the Worker Does
carpenter	makes things with wood
_____	delivers mail
hairdresser	cuts people's _____
_____	works with computers

B Look at the chart in A. Complete the sentences.

1. A _____ makes things with wood.
2. A _____ delivers mail.
3. A _____ works with computers.
4. A _____ cuts people's hair.

C Work with a partner. Talk about the jobs people have. Look at page 21 in the *Dictionary*. Use the chart in A. Take turns. Keep going.

A: What does a mechanic do?

B: A mechanic fixes cars.

B: What does a mail carrier do?

A: A mail carrier _____.

47

People at Work
Read and Connect

D Read about what some people do at work.

People at Work

1 People work every day of the week. People do many different kinds of work.

2 Today, some people are building a new building. A construction worker uses a drill. An electrician connects wires and switches. A carpenter builds things with wood.

3 Other people are working outside. A mail carrier delivers mail to homes and businesses. One firefighter cleans the fire truck. A police officer is in the street. She directs traffic. A mechanic works on a car. Mechanics fix cars or other machines.

4 Many people work inside buildings. A computer programmer spends many hours at a computer. A writer writes a book. On the third floor, a dentist takes care of a patient's teeth. A dental assistant helps the dentist. A hairdresser cuts a person's hair. A plumber fixes a sink in the same room.

5 On the first floor, a pharmacist and a salesperson work in the pharmacy. The pharmacist puts medicine in bottles. The salesperson helps a customer.

6 There are many jobs in the city. What job do you want to have?

1. Read the questions. Find and <u>underline</u> the answers in the reading.
   a. What does the electrician do?
   b. Who writes a book?
   c. What does the pharmacist do?
   d. What does the firefighter do?

2. Complete the sentences.
   a. The information about the police officer is in paragraph ___.
   b. The information about the dentist is in paragraph ___.
   c. The information about the salesperson is in paragraph ___.
   d. The information about the carpenter is in paragraph ___.

3. What is the main idea?
   a. The main idea is in paragraph ___.
   b. The main idea is _____
   _____
   _____

People at Work
Post-reading

E Work with a partner. Partner A: Say a sentence about the reading in D. Partner B: Is the sentence *true* or *false*? Make false sentences true. Take turns. Keep going.

A: The police officer works inside.

B: False. The police officer works _____.

B: The writer works in an office building.

A: _____

A: The construction worker _____.

B: _____

F Look at the picture. Complete the paragraph.

At the Pharmacy

Four people are working in the pharmacy today. The _____ is getting some medicine ready. A _____ is helping a shopper find bandages. A _____ is _____.

_____
_____
_____
_____

Topic 10 Word and Picture Cards

mail carrier	carpenter	electrician	construction worker
messenger	mechanic	police officer	firefighter
writer	computer programmer	painter	musician
plumber	hairdresser	dental assistant	dentist
pharmacist	salesperson		

Topic 10 Word and Picture Cards

TOPIC 11

The United States and U.S. Territories

Pre-reading

A Complete the chart. Use the words in the box. Tell where some places are located in the United States.

> New York   Arizona   South

The United States

State or City	Region of the U.S.
District of Columbia	East
Florida	_____
_____	Southwest
_____	Northeast

B Look at the chart in A. Complete the sentences.

1. The District of Columbia is in the _____.
2. _____ is in the Southwest.
3. Florida is in the _____.
4. _____ is in the Northeast.

C Work with a partner. Talk about the United States. Look at page 25 in the *Dictionary*. Use the chart in A. Take turns. Keep going.

A: Where is Indiana?

B: Indiana is south of _____.

B: What state is west of Utah?

A: _____ is west of Utah.

Name _____

TOPIC 11: The United States and U.S. Territories
Read and Connect

D Read about the United States.

The United States

1. The United States of America is a large country with many states and territories. There are 50 states in the United States. There are also five U.S. territories. The capital of the U.S. is the District of Columbia.

2. The largest state is Alaska. Alaska is far north of the other states. It is west of Canada. Texas is very large, too. It is east of New Mexico. Montana and Wyoming are two more large states.

3. There are many small states in the Northeast. Vermont is in the Northeast. It is smaller than any western state. Connecticut is even smaller. Rhode Island is the smallest state in the U.S.

4. California and Arizona are in the West. Florida is in the South. Hawaii is in the Pacific Ocean. It is very far south.

5. All of the U.S. territories are south of the United States. Puerto Rico and the U.S. Virgin Islands are south and east of the United States. Guam, American Samoa, and the Commonwealth of the Northern Mariana Islands are very far south. They are close to Australia.

6. There are many states in the United States. There are many territories, too. Where do you live?

1. **Read the questions. Find and <u>underline</u> the answers in the reading.**
   a. How many states are in the United States?
   b. What part of the U.S. is Vermont in?
   c. What is the smallest state in the U.S.?
   d. Where is Alaska?

2. **Complete the sentences.**
   a. The information about the largest states is in paragraph ___.
   b. The information about U.S. territories is in paragraph ___.
   c. The information about small states is in paragraph ___.
   d. The information about the U.S. capital is in paragraph ___.

3. **What is the main idea?**
   a. The main idea is in paragraph ___.
   b. The main idea is _____
   _____
   _____

Name _____

The United States and U.S. Territories
Post-reading

E Work with a partner. Partner A: Say a sentence about the reading in D. Partner B: Is the sentence *true* or *false*? Make false sentences true. Take turns. Keep going.

A: Vermont and Connecticut are large states.

B: _____. Vermont and Connecticut are _____ states.

B: Alaska is _____ of the other states.

A: _____

A: _____

B: _____

F Make a chart about where you live. Name the state or territory you live in. List the states or places north, south, east, and west of you.

Where I Live: _____

Place	Where It Is
_____	North of my home
_____	South of my home
_____	East of my home
_____	West of my home

G Use the chart in F. Write about the place you live.

Where I Live

I live in _____. It is a _____. It is in the _____ of the U.S. _____ is the closest state to the north.

_____

_____

_____

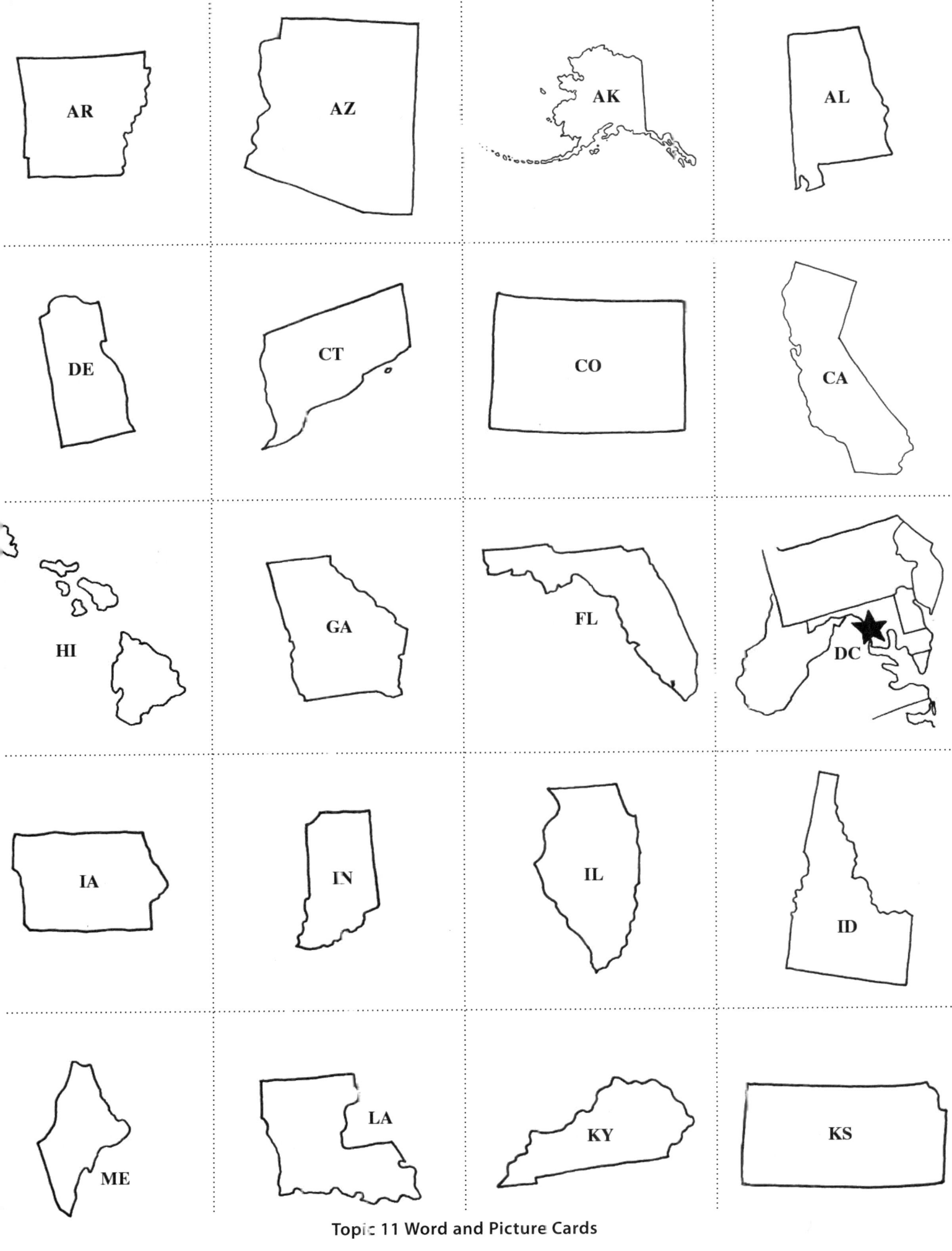
Topic 11 Word and Picture Cards

Alabama	Alaska	Arizona	Arkansas
California	Colorado	Connecticut	Delaware
District of Columbia	Florida	Georgia	Hawaii
Idaho	Illinois	Indiana	Iowa
Kansas	Kentucky	Louisiana	Maine

Topic 11 Word and Picture Cards

Maryland	Massachusetts	Michigan	Minnesota
Mississippi	Missouri	Montana	Nebraska
Nevada	New Hampshire	New Jersey	New Mexico
New York	North Carolina	North Dakota	Ohio
Oklahoma	Oregon	Pennsylvania	Rhode Island

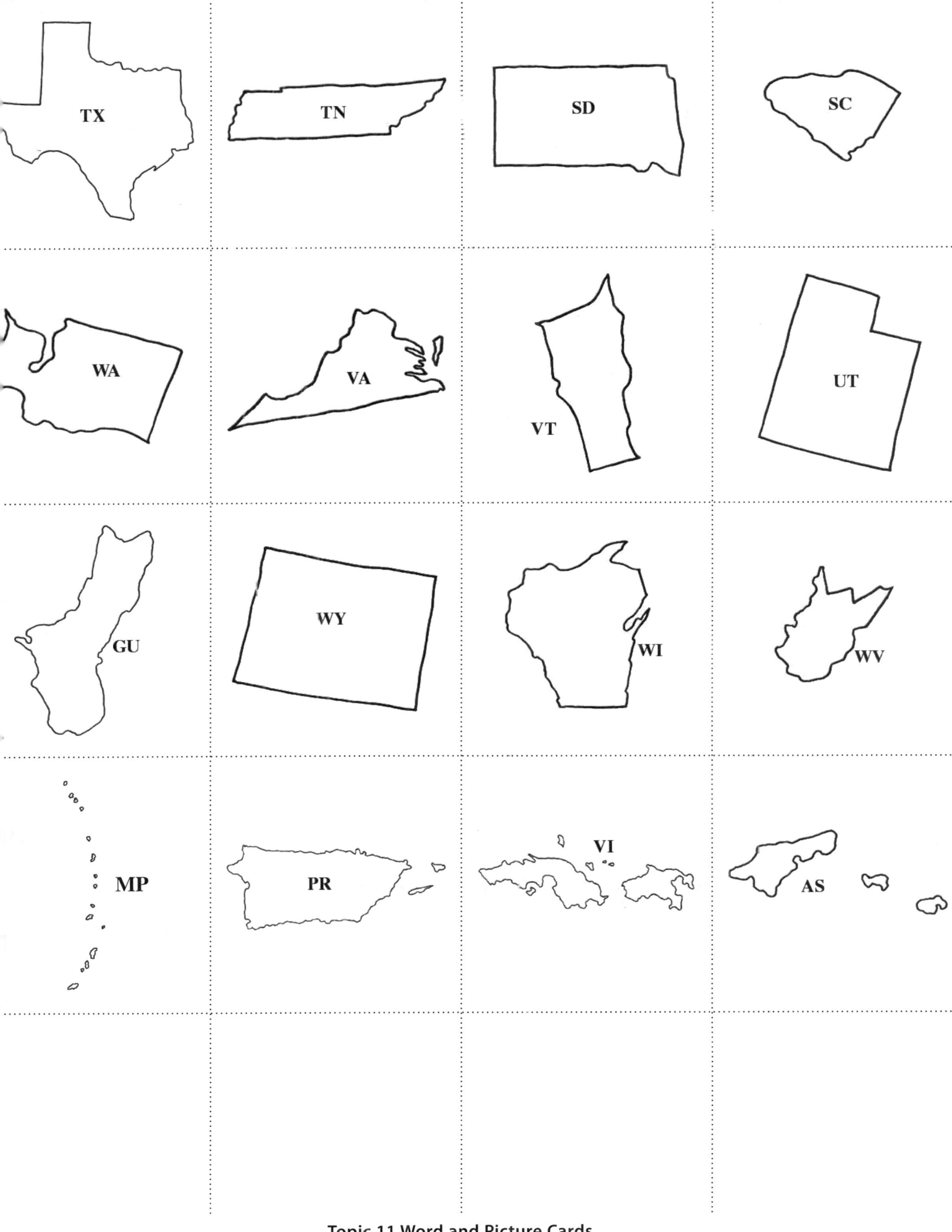

Topic 11 Word and Picture Cards

| South Carolina | South Dakota | Tennessee | Texas |

| Utah | Vermont | Virginia | Washington |

| West Virginia | Wisconsin | Wyoming | Guam |

| American Samoa | U.S. Virgin Islands | Puerto Rico | Commonwealth of the Northern Mariana Islands |

Topic 11 Word and Picture Cards

TOPIC 12

The Northeast

Pre-reading

A Complete the idea web. Use the words in the box. What is important in the Northeast?

> Statue of Liberty   stock market   television

(Idea web: The Northeast — Communication (satellite, newspaper, _____), Landmarks (Liberty Bell, The White House, Statue of Liberty), Finance (stocks and bonds, _____))

B Look at the idea web in A. Complete the sentences.

1. The Statue of Liberty is a _____.
2. Finance includes stocks and _____.
3. Newspapers are part of the _____ industry.
4. The Liberty Bell is a landmark in the _____.

C Work with a partner. Talk about the Northeast. Look at page 27 in the *Dictionary*. Use the idea web in A. Take turns. Keep going.

A: What are satellites used for?

B: Satellites are used for _____.

B: Where is the White House located?

A: It is located in the _____.

TOPIC 12 The Northeast
Read and Connect

D Read about the Northeast.

The Northeast

1   The Northeast is an important region. There are eleven states in the Northeast. The District of Columbia is in the Northeast, too.

2   Many finance businesses are located in the Northeast. People in finance work with money. Some people work in banks. Other people work in the stock market. They buy and sell stocks and bonds.

3   The communication industry is also in the Northeast. People in this industry share information with other people. Newscasters report the news in television studios. Writers report the news in newspapers and magazines. Newspaper headlines and advertisements give more information. Radios, telephones, and satellites are important, too. They carry information around the world.

4   There are famous landmarks in the Northeast, too. The Statue of Liberty is in New York City. The Liberty Bell is in Philadelphia. The White House is in the District of Columbia. These are important landmarks.

1. **Read the questions. Find and <u>underline</u> the answers in the reading.**
   a. What do newscasters do?
   b. What do people in finance do?
   c. How many states are in the Northeast?
   d. Where is the White House?

2. **Complete the sentences.**
   a. The information about newscasters is in paragraph ___.
   b. The information about the finance industry is in paragraph ___.
   c. The information about famous landmarks is in paragraph ___.

3. **What is the main idea?**
   a. The main idea is in paragraph ___.
   b. The main idea is _____
   _____
   _____

Name _____

TOPIC 12 The Northeast
Post-reading

E Work with a partner. Partner A: Say a sentence about the reading in D. Partner B: Is the sentence *true* or *false*? Make false sentences true. Take turns. Keep going.

A: A newscaster reports in the stock market.

B: False. A newscaster reports in a _____.

B: The _____ is in New York City.

A: True. The _____ is in New York City.

A: Headlines are part of _____.

B: _____

F Look at the picture. Complete the paragraph.

News in the Northeast

It is time for the news. People who report the news work in a _____.
A person operates the camera. A _____ reads the news. _____
_____
_____
_____

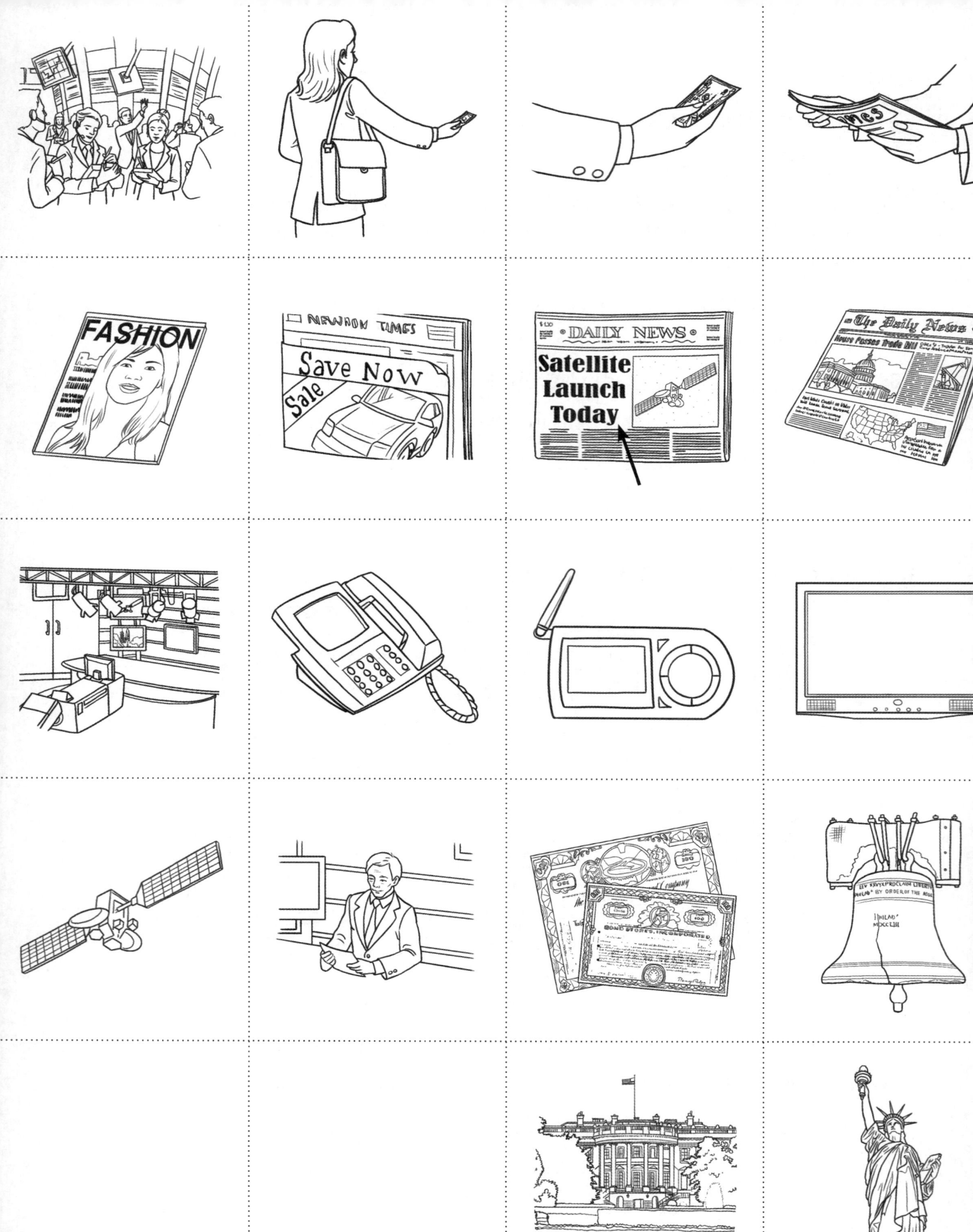

Topic 12 Word and Picture Cards

| sell | buy | businessperson | stock market |

| newspaper | headline | advertisement | magazine |

| television | radio | telephone | studio |

| Liberty Bell | stocks and bonds | newscaster | satellite |

| Statue of Liberty | White House | | |

Topic 12 Word and Picture Cards

TOPIC 13: The South

Pre-reading

A Complete the sequence chart. Use the words in the box. How do people get sugar or furniture?

> crop   lumber   sugar   furniture

From Raw Materials to Goods

	Sugar	Furniture
First	A farmer grows sugarcane.	Some people cut down trees.
Next	He harvests the _____ of sugarcane.	Workers cut the trees into _____.
Then	He sends the sugarcane to a factory.	Other workers shape the pieces of lumber.
Later	Workers make sugar from the sugarcane.	Other workers put the pieces of wood together.
Last	Trucks take the _____ to stores.	The finished _____ goes to stores.

B Look at the chart in A. Complete the sentences.

1. First, a farmer grows _____.
2. Then, he sends it to a _____.
3. Workers cut the trees into _____.
4. Last, the finished _____ goes to stores.

C Work with a partner. Talk about the South. Look at page 29 in the *Dictionary*. Use the chart in A. Take turns. Keep going.

A: What is the second step to make sugar?

B: The farmer harvests the _____.

B: What is the last step to get sugar?

A: Trucks take the _____ to stores.

66   ©Oxford University Press 2010. Limited permission granted to photocopy.

TOPIC 13 The South

Read and Connect

D Read about the South.

The South

1. There are twelve states in the South. These states manufacture many kinds of foods and goods.

2. Manufacturing is important in the South. Workers make many foods and goods from raw materials. Crops like sugarcane, cotton, and rice are raw materials. Lumber is also a raw material.

3. One important product is sugar. Where does the sugar come from? First, a farmer grows sugarcane. Next, he harvests the sugarcane crop. Then, he sends it to a factory. Later, workers make sugar from the sugarcane. Last, trucks take the sugar to stores.

4. Furniture is an important good, too. First, special workers cut down trees. Next, other workers cut the trees into lumber. Then, factory workers cut the lumber into many different shapes. Later, workers put the pieces of wood together. Last, the finished furniture goes to stores.

5. Manufacturing foods and goods takes a lot of people. Everyone at a factory's assembly line has a special job. They work together to make many things that we use every day.

1. **Read the questions. Find and underline the answers in the reading.**
   a. What do workers make from raw materials?
   b. Who puts the pieces of wood together?
   c. What is the first step to make sugar?
   d. How many states are in the South?

2. **Complete the sentences.**
   a. The information about sugar is in paragraph ___.
   b. The information about raw materials is in paragraph ___.
   c. The information about furniture is in paragraph ___.
   d. The information about states in the South is in paragraph ___.

3. **What is the main idea?**
   a. The main idea is in paragraph ___.
   b. The main idea is _____
   _____
   _____

Name _____

The South
Post-reading

E Work with a partner. Partner A: Say a sentence about the reading in D. Partner B: Is the sentence *true* or *false*? Make false sentences true. Take turns. Keep going.

A: There are six states in the South.

B: False. There are _____ states in the South.

B: The first step in making _____ is to cut down trees.

A: True. The first step is to cut down trees.

A: Sugar is made from _____.

B: _____

F Complete the sequence chart about how cotton is made into goods.

Cotton

First	Farmers grow cotton.
Next	They harvest the _____ of cotton.
Then	The cotton is sent to a _____.
Later	Workers make cloth and thread from the cotton.
Last	The cloth is sent to _____ and businesses.

G Use the sequence chart in F. Write about how cotton becomes a manufactured good.

Cotton

Making cotton cloth takes many steps. First, a farmer grows _____ plants. Next, the farmer harvests the crop. Then, the crop is _____. Later, workers make _____

_____

_____

Topic 13 Word and Picture Cards

sugarcane	cotton	rice	crop
sugar	factory	worker	assembly line
lumber	cloth	thread	furniture
raw materials	goods	port	plantation
Mississippi River	Kennedy Space Center		

Topic 13 Word and Picture Cards

TOPIC 14

The Midwest

Pre-reading

A Fill in the chart. Use the words in the box. What things can be on farms in the Midwest?

> farmhouse   plow   wheat

In the Midwest

Farm Products	Farm Buildings	Farm Machines
cattle	dairy barn	combine
corn	_____	_____
soybeans	grain elevator	
_____		

B Look at the chart in A. Complete the sentences.

1. A dairy _____ is a kind of farm building.
2. A combine is a kind of _____.
3. Crops like soybeans, _____, and corn are farm products.
4. A _____ elevator is a kind of farm building.

C Work with a partner. Talk about the Midwest. Look at page 31 in the *Dictionary*. Use the chart in A. Take turns. Keep going.

A: What do farmers use combines for?

B: Farmers use combines to _____ grain.

B: What are _____?

A: _____ are _____.

Name _____

TOPIC 14

The Midwest
Read and Connect

D Read about the Midwest.

The Midwest

1   The Midwest is in the middle of the United States. There are twelve states in the Midwest. Six Midwest states are near the Great Lakes. Six states are in the Great Plains. The Midwest states have flat land and low hills. Agriculture is very important in the Midwest.

2   Agriculture means farming. Many farmers raise cattle, or cows. Other farmers grow soybeans. Many farmers grow grain, such as wheat and corn.

3   How do farmers grow grain? They use special farm machines. Farmers turn the soil with plows. Then, they plant the seeds. The plants grow all summer. Later, the farmers use a combine to harvest the grain. They keep some hay to feed to cattle. They take the grain to a grain elevator to store the grain. The grain is used for many foods, like bread.

4   Dairy farming is also important in the Midwest. Many farmers raise dairy cattle for milk. They send the milk to a factory. Then, some of the milk becomes cheese or yogurt. Some of the milk goes to supermarkets.

5   Agriculture is an important industry in the Midwest. Much of the United States' food comes from this region. What foods do you eat that come from the Midwest?

1. **Read the questions. Find and <u>underline</u> the answers in the reading.**
   a. What do farmers use to turn the soil?
   b. How many states are in the Great Plains?
   c. What is the grain used for?

2. **Complete the sentences.**
   a. The information about harvesting grain is in paragraph ___.
   b. The information about soybeans is in paragraph ___.
   c. The information about states near the Great Lakes is in paragraph ___.
   d. The information about dairy farming is in paragraph ___.

3. **What is the main idea?**
   a. The main idea is in paragraph ___.
   b. The main idea is _____
   _____
   _____

TOPIC 14 The Midwest
Post-reading

E Work with a partner. Partner A: Say a sentence about the reading in D. Partner B: Is the sentence *true* or *false*? Make false sentences true. Take turns. Keep going.

A: Farmers in the Midwest grow soybeans, _____, and corn.

B: True. These crops grow in the Midwest.

B: The Great Plains states have tall mountains.

A: _____. They have _____.

A: _____

B: _____

F Make a chart about what farms produce in your state.

Farms in My State

Farm Crops	Farm Animals	Farm Products

G Use the chart in F. Write about farms products in your state.

Farms in My State

I live in _____. Some farmers in my state grow _____.

Some of the _____ is/are used to make _____. Other

farmers in my state raise _____.

_____

_____

_____

Topic 14 Word and Picture Cards

dairy barn	cattle	farmhouse	plant
harvest	plow	combine	hay
wheat	soybeans	corn	grain
grain elevator	Great Lakes	Great Plains	Mount Rushmore

TOPIC 15

The Mountain West

Pre-reading

A Complete the chart. Use the words in the box. What things can people see in the Mountain West?

> minerals   Old Faithful   cowgirls

The Mountain West

Mines	Ranches	Famous Places
open pit mines	corrals	Continental Divide
_____	livestock	_____
ore	_____	Rocky Mountains
		Yellowstone National Park

B Look at the chart in A. Complete the sentences.

1. Ore is a special kind of rock found in a _____.
2. Livestock are animals that live on a _____.
3. A famous place in the Mountain West is _____ National Park.
4. The Continental _____ is a famous place in the Mountain West.

C Work with a partner. Talk about the Mountain West. Look at page 33 in the *Dictionary*. Use the chart in A. Take turns. Keep going.

A: What kind of mines can you see in the Mountain West?

B: You can see _____ mines in the Mountain West.

B: Where can you see cowboys and _____?

A: You can see them working on a _____.

TOPIC 15

The Mountain West
Read and Connect

D Read about the Mountain West.

The Mountain West

1   The Mountain West has five states. They are Idaho, Montana, Wyoming, Utah, and Colorado. People started ranches in these states in the 1800s. Many other people started mines. The Mountain West has many important natural features that people use.

2   The Rocky Mountains are in these states. The mountains have many high peaks. The Continental Divide is in the Rocky Mountains. All rivers west of the Continental Divide flow west. All rivers east of the Divide flow east and north.

3   Many people come to the Mountain West to find ore. Ore is a kind of rock that has minerals in it. Copper and silver are two kinds of minerals. People use them to make coins and jewelry. People dig mines to get the ore. Some mines are big open pits.

4   Ranchers raise cattle and horses on ranches. Cowboys and cowgirls work on ranches, too.

5   You can see wild bison in Yellowstone National Park. People visit Yellowstone to see wild animals and geysers. Old Faithful is the most famous geyser. It shoots hot water and steam high into the air many times a day.

1. **Read the questions. Find and <u>underline</u> the answers in the reading.**
   a. What states are in the Mountain West?
   b. What can people use minerals for?
   c. Why is Old Faithful famous?
   d. Why do people dig mines?

2. **Complete the sentences.**
   a. The information about the Rocky Mountains is in paragraph ___.
   b. The information about ranchers is in paragraph ___.
   c. The information about the Continental Divide is in paragraph ___.
   d. The information about ore is in paragraph ___.

3. **What is the main idea?**
   a. The main idea is in paragraph ___.
   b. The main idea is _____
   _____
   _____

Name _____

The Mountain West
Post-reading

E Work with a partner. Partner A: Say a sentence about the reading in D. Partner B: Is the sentence *true* or *false*? Make false sentences true. Take turns. Keep going.

A: People dig open pits to get hot water.

B: False. People dig open pits to find _____.

B: Cowboys and cowgirls work on _____.

A: True. They work on _____.

A: _____

B: _____

F Look at the picture. Complete the paragraph.

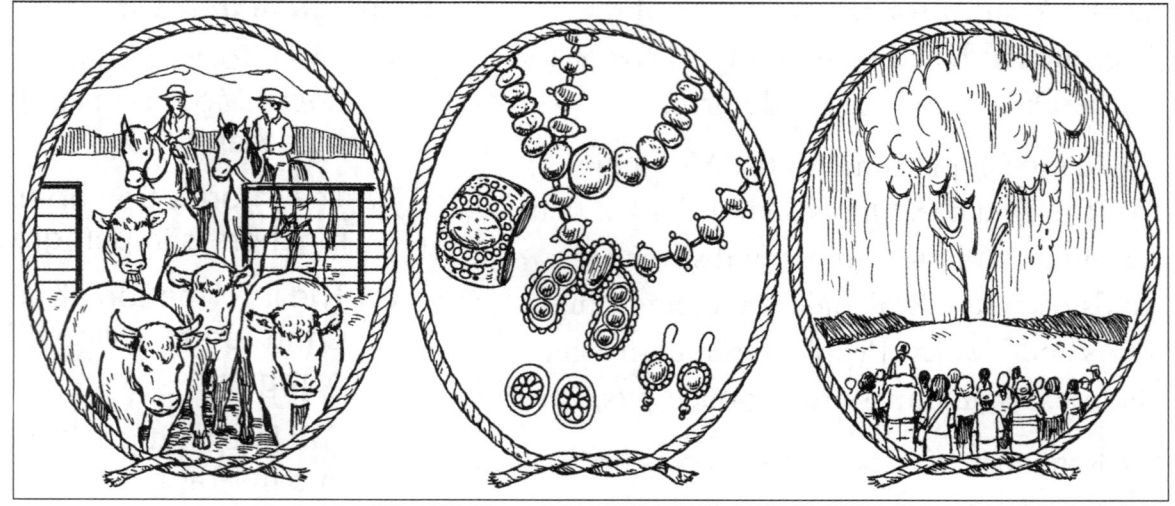

The Mountain West

Many people come to the Mountain West. Some are cowboys or _____ _____. They work on _____. People use _____ to make jewelry. _____

_____

_____

Topic 15 Word and Picture Cards

open pit	mine	ore	minerals
ranch	livestock	corral	cowgirl
cowboy	bison	herd	graze
Rocky Mountains	peak	Continental Divide	rodeo
Yellowstone National Park	Old Faithful		

Topic 15 Word and Picture Cards

TOPIC 16

The Northwest

Pre-reading

A Complete the chart. Use the words in the box. How do people get wood? How do they catch fish?

> boat   fish   sawmill   nets

Working in the Northwest

	Logging	Fishing
First	Lumberjacks cut down trees.	First, the fishermen go fishing in a _____.
Next	The timber goes to a _____.	Next, the fishermen catch many fish in _____.
Then	Then the timber is cut into boards.	Then some fish go to a cannery.
Last	Carpenters build things with the boards.	People buy the _____ in supermarkets.

B Look at the chart in A. Complete the sentences.

1. _____, lumberjacks cut down trees.
2. Next, the timber goes to a _____.
3. Fishermen use _____ to catch fish.
4. People buy _____ in supermarkets.

C Work with a partner. Talk about the Northwest. Look at page 35 in the *Dictionary*. Use the chart in A. Take turns. Keep going.

A: What do fishermen do after they catch fish?

B: They take the fish to a _____.

B: What do lumberjacks do first?

A: They cut trees in the _____.

©Oxford University Press 2010. Limited permission granted to photocopy.

TOPIC 16

The Northwest
Read and Connect

D Read about the Northwest.

The Northwest

1   Alaska, Washington, and Oregon are in the Northwest. The Northwest has many forests and a lot of water. That is why logging and fishing are important in the Northwest.

2   The Northwest gets a lot of rain. The rainfall helps redwood and pine trees grow well. Lumberjacks cut down some of these trees. Sometimes they help plan where to plant new trees, too.

3   People build things with wood from the trees. How do they get the wood? First, lumberjacks cut down trees with chain saws. Next, the timber goes to a sawmill. Then, the wood is cut into boards. The sawdust can become wood products, too. Finally, people buy the wood and build things with it.

4   Many people like to eat fish. How do they get the fish? First, fishermen use boats and nets to catch fish. Next, some of the fish go to a cannery. Then, the fish is packed in cans. Next, the cans of fish are taken to stores. Finally, people buy and eat the fish.

5   The Northwest has many resources that people need. It takes many steps to get these resources from nature to stores.

1. **Find the sequence words in the reading. Underline *first*, *next*, *then*, and *finally*.**
2. **Complete the sentences.**
   a. The information about rainfall is in paragraph ___.
   b. The information about sawmills is in paragraph ___.
   c. The information about the redwoods and pine trees is in paragraph ___.
   d. The information about canneries is in paragraph ___.
3. **What is the main idea?**
   a. The main idea is in paragraph ___.
   b. The main idea is _____
   _____
   _____

TOPIC 16

The Northwest

Post-reading

E Work with a partner. Partner A: Say a sentence about the reading in D. Partner B: Is the sentence *true* or *false*? Make false sentences true. Take turns. Keep going.

A: There is a lot of rainfall in the Northwest.

B: True. The Northwest has a lot of rainfall.

B: Fishermen cut down some of the trees.

A: False. _____ cut down some of the trees.

A: Rainfall helps pine trees and _____ grow well.

B: _____

F Look at the picture. Complete the paragraph.

A Visit to a Famous Place

Gita's family goes to visit the Space Needle in Seattle. First, they drive there. _____, they buy tickets. Then, _____.

_____

_____

Topic 16 Word and Picture Cards

forest	logging	lumberjack	chain saw
redwood	pine	timber	sawmill
wood	sawdust	fish	cannery
boat	net	rainfall	Puget Sound
Space Needle	Alaska Pipeline		

Topic 16 Word and Picture Cards

TOPIC 17

The Southwest

Pre-reading

A Complete the chart. Use the words in the box. What words describe natural resources?

> dam   hydroelectric   well   irrigation

Natural Resources in the Southwest

Water	Oil	Electricity
reservoir	drill	_____ plant
_____ canal	refinery	
water storage	_____	
_____	pipeline	

B Look at the chart in A. Complete the sentences.

1. People use drills to get _____.
2. People use an irrigation _____ to move water.
3. A _____ makes gasoline and other things from oil.
4. A hydroelectric plant is a source of _____.

C Work with a partner. Talk about the Southwest. Look at page 37 in the *Dictionary*. Use the chart in A. Take turns. Keep going.

A: Is land an important natural resource in the Southwest?
B: Yes, it is.
B: Which resource goes through pipelines?
A: _____ goes through pipelines.

Name _____

TOPIC 17

The Southwest
Read and Connect

D Read about the Southwest.

The Southwest

1   Natural resources are things we need but cannot make. They only come from nature. Water, land, and oil are natural resources. In the Southwest, some natural resources are easy to find. Others are hard to find. Natural resources are very important in the Southwest.

2   Oil and natural gas are deep in the ground. People use drills to make wells. Pipelines move the oil from wells. The pipelines take oil and gas to refineries. People use the oil to make gasoline and other things. Pipelines also take natural gas to people's homes. People use natural gas to heat their homes.

3   The Southwest is usually hot and dry. A cactus doesn't need much water. But people must have water. People build dams and irrigation canals. Dams make reservoirs by holding water from rivers. Irrigation canals take water to farms.

4   People also need electricity. We use natural resources to make electricity. Hydroelectric plants use water from dams to make electricity. Falling water turns machines. The machines make electricity.

5   The Southwest has many natural resources. People work hard to get these important resources.

1. **Read the questions. Find and <u>underline</u> the answers in the reading.**
   a. What do hydroelectric plants do?
   b. Where are oil and nature gas found?
   c. Why do people use natural gas?
   d. How do dams make reservoirs?

2. **Complete the sentences.**
   a. The information about irrigation canals is in paragraph ___.
   b. The information about pipelines is in paragraph ___.
   c. The information about hydroelectric plants is in paragraph ___.

3. **What is the main idea?**
   a. The main idea is in paragraph ___.
   b. The main idea is _____
   _____

TOPIC 17

The Southwest
Post-reading

E Work with a partner. Partner A: Say a sentence about the reading in D. Partner B: Is the sentence *true* or *false*? Make false sentences true. Take turns. Keep going.

A: People build dams to store oil.

B: False. People build dams to store _____.

B: The Southwest is usually cold and wet.

A: False. The Southwest is usually _____.

A: Hydroelectric plants _____.

B: _____.

F Look at the picture. Complete the paragraph.

Living in the Southwest

People need many natural resources. In the Southwest, there is little _____. _____ bring water to farms and cities.

_____

_____

_____

Topic 17 Word and Picture Cards

drill	natural gas	oil	well
gasoline	tank	pipeline	refinery
irrigation canal	reservoir	dam	water storage
cactus	Grand Canyon	electricity	hydroelectric plant

TOPIC 18

The West Coast and Pacific

Pre-reading

A Complete the chart. Use the words in the box. What are some important businesses in the West Coast and Pacific states?

> movie camera   laser   surfing

The West Coast and Pacific

Technology	Tourism	Entertainment
fiber optics	Golden Gate Bridge	actor and actress
_____	resort	_____
microchip	shopping mall	director
	_____	filmmaking
	tourist	script
		set

B Look at the chart in A. Complete the sentences.

1. Filmmaking is part of the _____ industry.
2. Tourists come to California to see the _____ Bridge.
3. Some workers in the _____ industry use lasers.
4. _____ stay in resorts.

C Work with a partner. Talk about the West Coast and Pacific. Look at page 39 in the *Dictionary*. Use the chart in A. Take turns. Keep going.

A: What industry makes microchips?
B: The technology industry makes microchips.
B: What do both actresses and _____ read?
A: Both actresses and _____ read _____.

TOPIC 18: The West Coast and Pacific

Read and Connect

D Read about the West Coast and Pacific.

The West Coast and Pacific

1   California is on the west coast of the United States. Hawaii is in the Pacific Ocean. Technology, tourism, and entertainment are some important businesses in these states.

2   Many people enjoy movies. Movies and filmmaking are part of the entertainment industry. Hollywood, California, is called the filmmaking capital of the U.S. Many people work in filmmaking. Both actors and actresses make movies. They work on sets. They read scripts. Directors tell them what to do. Workers record movies with movie cameras.

3   Technology is important in California, too. People work with both lasers and fiber optics. People also make microchips. Microchips are important parts in computers.

4   Tourism is important in both Hawaii and California. Many tourists come to see the beautiful beaches and resorts. They enjoy both surfing and swimming.

5   Many tourists come to California. Some of them come to see the Golden Gate Bridge. Other tourists visit shopping malls.

6   Imagine a trip to California or Hawaii. What do you want to see?

1. Read the questions. Find and <u>underline</u> the answers in the reading.
    a. What city is called the filmmaking capital of the U.S.?
    b. What do actors and actresses make?
    c. What do people in technology work with?
    d. Where is tourism important?

2. Complete the sentences.
    a. The information about the entertainment industry is in paragraph ___.
    b. The information about beaches is in paragraph ___.
    c. The information about what tourists see in California is in paragraph ___.
    d. The information about microchips is in paragraph ___.

3. What is the main idea?
    a. The main idea is in paragraph ___.
    b. The main idea is _____
    _____
    _____

TOPIC 18 The West Coast and Pacific

Post-reading

E Work with a partner. Partner A: Say a sentence about the reading in D. Partner B: Is the sentence *true* or *false*? Make false sentences true. Take turns. Keep going.

A: Microchips come from the technology industry.

B: True. Microchips are technology.

B: A resort is part of the technology industry.

A: _____. A resort is part of the _____ industry.

A: _____

B: _____

F Look at the picture. Complete the paragraph.

Our Movie

Our class made a movie about famous scientists. One student was the _____. She told the actor and _____ what to do. Another student operated the movie _____. _____

_____

_____

_____

Topic 18 Word and Picture Cards

actress	actor	filmmaking	set
fiber optics	movie camera	director	script
surfing	tourist	resort	laser
Golden Gate Bridge	shopping mall	freeway	microchip

TOPIC 19

Canada and Mexico

Pre-reading

A Complete the Venn diagram. Use the words in the box. How are Canada and Mexico the same? How are they different?

> states   money   national border   provinces

Canada and Mexico

- Canada: _____ / territories
- (overlap) capital city / _____
- Mexico: _____ / silver

B Look at the Venn diagram in A. Complete the sentences.

1. Both Canada and Mexico have a _____ with the U.S.
2. Only _____ has states.
3. Both Canada and Mexico have a _____ city.
4. Only Canada has provinces and _____.

C Work with a partner. Talk about Canada and Mexico. Look at page 41 of the *Dictionary*. Use the Venn diagram in A. Take turns. Keep going.

A: On both maps what does a star represent?

B: A star represents a _____ on both maps.

B: Which map has a symbol that represents _____?

A: The map of _____ has a symbol that represents _____.

TOPIC 19

Canada and Mexico

Read and Connect

D Read about the Canada and Mexico maps on *Dictionary* page 41.

Map Symbols for Canada and Mexico

1. The United States has two neighbors. These countries are Canada and Mexico. The maps show important information about Canada and Mexico.

2. Most maps have a compass rose. It shows the directions north, south, east, and west. Canada is the country to the north of the United States. Mexico is the country to the south.

3. The colors, lines, and shapes on a map are symbols. Each symbol represents a different thing. A map legend explains what the symbols represent. For example, the red line represents a national border. A national border is where two countries touch.

4. Most maps have lines. Some lines go from north to south. These are lines of longitude. Other lines go from east to west. These are lines of latitude. Together these lines help people find places on the map.

5. Maps can show a lot of fun and important information. Which country has totem poles? Which one has pyramids and silver? Do you see the money and flag of each country?

1. Read the questions. Find and <u>underline</u> the answers in the reading.
   a. What countries are neighbors to the United States?
   b. How do the lines of latitude and longitude help people?
   c. What explains the meaning of symbols on a map?
   d. What do the two maps show?

2. Complete the sentences.
   a. The information about latitude and longitude is in paragraph ___.
   b. The information about national borders is in paragraph ___.
   c. The information about a compass rose is in paragraph ___.
   d. The information about map symbols is in paragraph ___.

3. What is the main idea?
   a. The main idea is in paragraph ___.
   b. The main idea is _____
   _____
   _____

Name _____

Canada and Mexico
Post-reading

E Work with a partner. Partner A: Say a sentence about the reading in D. Partner B: Is the sentence *true* or *false*? Make false sentences true. Take turns. Keep going.

A: A compass rose is a map.

B: False. A compass rose shows directions on a map.

B: A legend shows _____.

A: True. A legend shows _____.

A: _____

B: _____

F Look at the map. Complete the paragraph.

Favorite Sports in Mexico

This is a map of Mexico. There are three symbols on the map's _____. One symbol represents _____. Another symbol

_____

_____

_____

98

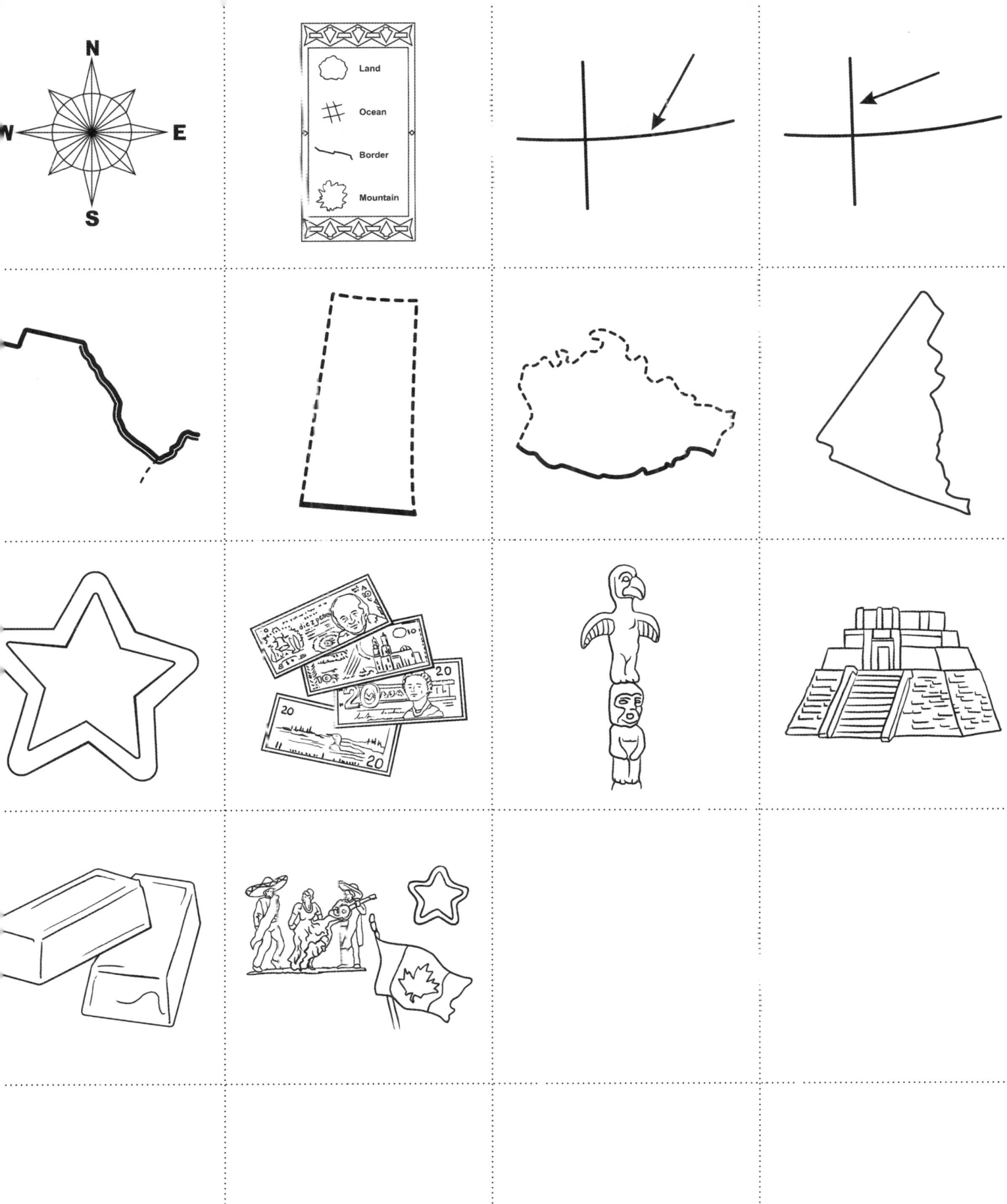

Topic 19 Word and Picture Cards

longitude	latitude	legend	compass rose
territory	state	province	national border
pyramid	totem pole	money	capital city
		symbols	silver

TOPIC 20

Europe, Russia, and the Independent Republics
Pre-reading

A Complete the chart. Use the names in the box. Which countries go in each region?

> Greece   Kazakhstan   Latvia   Sweden   Luxembourg

Countries in Europe and Central Asia

Scandinavia	Baltic Countries	Balkan Countries	Central Asian Republics	Benelux
Denmark	Estonia	Albania	_____	Belgium
Iceland	_____	Bosnia and Herzegovina	Kyrgyzstan	Netherlands
Finland	Lithuania	Bulgaria	Tajikistan	_____
Norway		Croatia	Turkmenistan	
_____		_____	Uzbekistan	
		Macedonia		
		Montenegro		
		Serbia		

B Look at the chart in A. Complete the sentences.

1. Serbia is one of the _____ countries.
2. Tajikistan and Uzbekistan are _____.
3. Finland is in _____.

C Work with a partner. Talk about countries and regions. Use the chart in A. Look at page 43 in the *Dictionary*. Take turns. Keep going.

A: What region is Macedonia in?

B: Macedonia is a _____ country.

B: Where is _____?

A: _____ is in _____.

101

Name _____

Europe, Russia, and the Independent Republics
Read and Connect

D Read about Europe, Russia, and the Independent Republics.

Europe, Russia, and the Independent Republics

1. Europe is a continent. A continent is a large part of the Earth's land. Europe is made of many different countries and regions.

2. Europe has many peninsulas. A peninsula is land with water on three sides of it. The Balkan Peninsula is located in Southeastern Europe. The Iberian Peninsula is in Western Europe. Scandinavia has many peninsulas and islands.

3. Twenty-seven countries in Europe are in the European Union. Some of these countries were part of the Soviet Union. The Soviet Union ruled many countries in Europe and Central Asia. It included Russia and the Baltic countries.

4. The Soviet Union ended in 1991. All the countries in it became independent republics. A republic is a country where the people choose their leaders.

5. Russia is the largest country in the world. Part of Russia is in Europe. Siberia is a huge area of land in Russia. It goes all the way across Asia to the Pacific Ocean.

6. The countries in each region have many things in common. All of these countries and regions make up the continent of Europe.

---

1. **Read the questions. Find and underline the answers in the reading.**
   a. What is a continent?
   b. How big is Russia?
   c. How many countries are in the European Union?
   d. What is Siberia?

2. **Complete the sentences.**
   a. The information about peninsulas is in paragraph ___.
   b. The information about continents is in paragraph ___.
   c. The information about Russia is in paragraph ___.
   d. The information about independent republics is in paragraph ___.

3. **What is the main idea?**
   a. The main idea is in paragraph ___.
   b. The main idea is _____
   _____
   _____

TOPIC 20

Europe, Russia, and the Independent Republics
Post-reading

E Work with a partner. Partner A: Say a sentence about the reading in D. Partner B: Is the sentence *true* or *false*? Make false sentences true. Take turns. Keep going.

A: Scandinavia has many peninsulas.

B: True. Scandinavia has many peninsulas.

B: Russia is a country in Scandinavia.

A: False. Russia is in _____.

A: The European Union _____.

B: _____.

F Make a chart about some regions and countries of Europe.

Regions of Europe

Western Europe	Central Europe	Eastern Europe

G Use the chart in F. Write about Europe.

Regions of Europe

There are many regions and countries in Europe. One country in Western Europe is _____. Another is _____. Two countries in Central Europe are _____

_____

_____

Topic 20 Word and Picture Cards

Benelux	Iberian Peninsula	Western Europe	European Union
Balkan countries	Mediterranean countries	Central Europe	Scandinavia
Siberia	Central Asian republics	Baltic countries	Eastern Europe

Topic 21: Asia, Africa, and Australia

Pre-reading

A Complete the chart. Use the words in the box. What are some important landmarks and religions?

> Taoism   Sahara   Uluru   Hinduism

Landmarks and Religions

Africa	Asia	Australia
Great Pyramid	Mount Everest	Great Barrier Reef
Nile River	Buddhism	_____
_____	Christianity	
Victoria Falls	Confucianism	
	_____	
	Islam	
	Judaism	
	_____	
	Sikhism	

B Look at the chart in A. Complete the sentences.

1. Mount Everest is in _____.
2. Hinduism started in _____.
3. The Great Pyramid is in _____.
4. The _____ Reef is near Australia.

C Work with a partner. Talk about Asia, Africa, and Australia. Look at page 45 in the *Dictionary*. Use the chart in A. Take turns. Keep going.

A: Where did Buddhism start?

B: Buddhism started in _____.

B: Where is _____?

A: _____ is in _____.

Asia, Africa, and Australia
Read and Connect

D Read about Asia, Africa, and Australia.

Asia, Africa, and Australia

1   Asia, Africa, and Australia are three of the world's continents. These continents are important for their religions and special places.

2   Asia is the largest continent. It is home to Mount Everest, the world's highest mountain. The world's most common religions all started in Asia. Hinduism is one of the world's oldest religions. It started in India. Sikhism and Buddhism also started there. Taoism and Confucianism started in China. Shinto began in Japan.

3   Some religions began in southwest Asia. Judaism and Christianity started in Israel. Islam started in Saudi Arabia.

4   Africa is the second largest continent. It has the world's longest river, the Nile River. The Great Pyramid is also in Africa. It is one of the largest things ever built by people.

5   Australia is another continent. A famous rock named Uluru is near the center of Australia. The Great Barrier Reef is in the ocean near Australia.

6   These continents have many important features. They also have much important history for the world's religions.

---

1. **Read the questions. Find and <u>underline</u> the answers in the reading.**
   a. What started in Saudi Arabia?
   b. Where did Hinduism start?
   c. Where is Uluru?
   d. Where is the Great Pyramid?

2. **Complete the sentences.**
   a. The information about the Nile River is in paragraph ___.
   b. The information about Africa is in paragraph ___.
   c. The information about Hinduism is in paragraph ___.
   d. The information about Mount Everest is in paragraph ___.

3. **What is the main idea?**
   a. The main idea is in paragraph ___.
   b. The main idea is _____
   _____

Name _____

TOPIC 21

Asia, Africa, and Australia
Post-reading

E Work with a partner. Partner A: Say a sentence about the reading in D. Partner B: Is the sentence *true* or *false*? Make false sentences true. Take turns. Keep going.

A: Christianity started in Asia.

B: True. It started in southwest Asia.

B: The Great Pyramid is in Australia.

A: _____. The Great Pyramid is in _____.

A: _____

B: _____

F Look at the pictures. Complete the paragraph.

 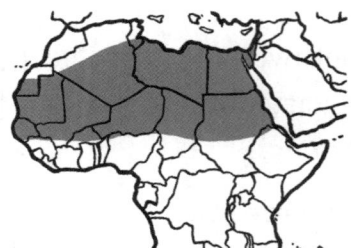 

Famous Places in Africa

Africa has many famous landmarks. The _____ is a large desert in north Africa. It is the largest hot desert in the world. The _____ are also in Africa. They are _____. The Nile River is _____.

_____
_____
_____

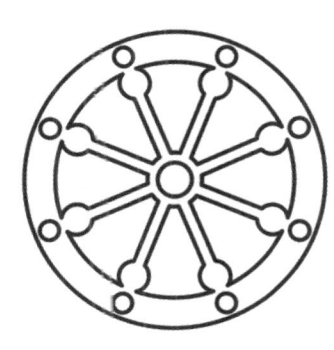

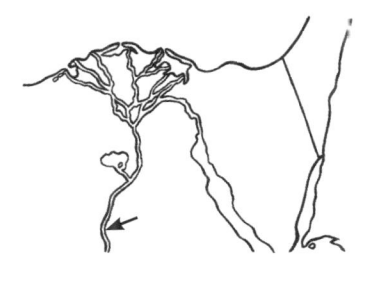
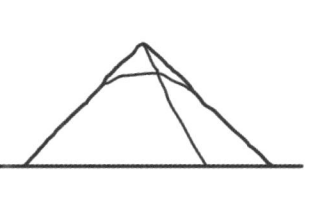
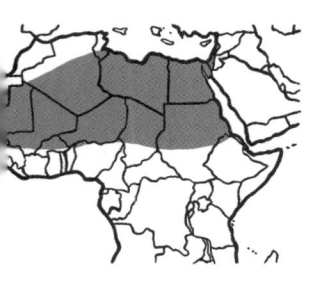

Topic 21 Word and Picture Cards

Sikhism	Mount Everest	Confucianism	Taoism
Islam	Shinto	Buddhism	Hinduism
Great Pyramid	Nile River	Judaism	Christianity
Great Barrier Reef	Uluru	Victoria Falls	Sahara

Central and South America and the Caribbean

Name _____

Pre-reading

A Complete the chart. Use the words in the box. Where were empires and cities located?

> Chichén Itzá   Machu Picchu   Tenochtitlán

Early Empires

Empire	Important Cities	Place
2000 BC – AD 900 Mayan Empire	_____	Central America
AD 1428 – AD 1521 Aztec Empire	_____	Central America
AD 1200 – AD 1532 Inca Empire	_____	South America

B Look at the chart in A. Complete the sentences.

1. The Mayan Empire started in _____.
2. _____ was an important Mayan city.
3. The Inca Empire ended in _____.
4. The _____ built Tenochtitlán.

C Work with a partner. Talk about Central and South America and the Caribbean. Look at page 47 in the *Dictionary*. Use the chart in A. Take turns. Keep going.

A: What was Machu Picchu?

B: Machu Picchu was an _____ city.

B: Where was the _____ Empire?

A: It was in _____.

Central and South America and the Caribbean
Read and Connect

D Read about Central and South America and the Caribbean.

Central and South America and the Caribbean

1   Long ago, three important empires formed in Central and South America. An empire has one ruler. An emperor controls the empire's people and land.

2   The Mayan Empire began in Central America about 2000 BC. The Mayans wrote with glyphs. Glyphs are pictures and shapes that people read like words. The Mayans built Chichén Itzá. The empire ended, but Mayan people still live in the region.

3   Around AD 1200, the Inca Empire began. Machu Picchu was an important Inca city. The Inca used quipus to record information. A quipu was a set of strings with knots.

4   The Aztec people built the city of Tenochtitlán in Mexico. Around 1428, the Aztec Empire began.

5   In 1492, Spanish conquistadors came to the Americas. They conquered, or controlled, the native people. In 1513, Balboa crossed Panama. He was the first European to see the Pacific Ocean. Cortés conquered the Aztecs in 1521. In 1532, Pizarro conquered the Inca.

6   The empires disappeared, but they left much history. Their cities and inventions are still famous today.

1. **Read the questions. Find and <u>underline</u> the answers in the reading.**
   a. How many empires were in Central and South America long ago?
   b. Which Spanish explorer first came to the Pacific Ocean?
   c. What did Pizarro do?
   d. Who used glyphs as a kind of writing?

2. **Complete the sentences.**
   a. The information about the Inca Empire is in paragraph ___.
   b. The information about the Aztec Empire is in paragraph ___.
   c. The information about conquistadors is in paragraph ___.

3. **What is the main idea?**
   a. The main idea is in paragraph ___.
   b. The main idea is _____

Central and South America and the Caribbean
Post-reading

E Work with a partner. Partner A: Say a sentence about the reading in D. Partner B: Is the sentence *true* or *false*? Make false sentences true. Take turns. Keep going.

A: The Inca Empire started in South America.

B: True.

B: A quipu was a kind of picture.

A: _____. A quipu was _____.

F Make a chart about the conquistadors.

Spanish Conquistadors

Explorer	When	What
Vasco Núñez de Balboa	1513	He was the first European to see the _____.
Hernán Cortés	1521	He and the Spanish conquered the _____.
_____	_____	He and the Spanish conquered the Inca.

G Use the chart in F. Write about what conquistadors did in Central and South America.

The Spanish Conquistadors

Spanish conquistadors came to Central and South America in the 1500s. They conquered the native people. _____ was the first European to see _____. _____ conquered _____.

_____

_____

_____

Topic 22 Word and Picture Cards

Hernán Cortés	Tenochtitlán	Moctezuma	Aztec calendar
Machu Picchu	Vasco Núñez de Balboa	Chichén Itzá	glyph
Atahualpa	Francisco Pizarro	conquistadors	quipu

Answer Key

Topic 1 The Classroom
pages 2–4

A

2 computers, 3 rulers, 4 crayons, 1 chalkboard, and 5 chairs

B

1. two
2. five
3. one
4. four

C

Accept all reasonable answers.

D1

a. Paragraph 2: There are ten students in the classroom.
b. Paragraph 4: A computer is on one of the tables, and another computer is on a desk. (two computers)
c. Paragraph 4: There is a clock on the wall. (one clock)
d. Paragraph 4: There is a flag in the classroom. (one flag)

D2

a. 4
b. 3
c. 3

D3

a. Paragraph 1
b. The main idea is there are people and many useful things in Anita's classroom.

E

B: False. There is one clock in the classroom.

Accept all reasonable answers.

F

Accept all reasonable answers.

G

Answers will vary but may include:
There are many people and things in my classroom. There are twelve students. There are six girls and there are six boys. There are twelve desks. There is one pencil sharpener. I have one pencil and one pen. I like my classroom.

Topic 2 The School
pages 7–9

A

First row: custodian
Second row: gym, library, office

B

1. gym
2. librarian
3. hall
4. secretary

C

Accept all reasonable answers.

D1

a. Paragraph 2: The students eat lunch in the cafeteria.
b. Paragraph 3: The water fountain is in the hall.
c. Paragraph 4: The librarian helps the students.
d. Paragraph 4: The media center is in the library.

D2

a. 3
b. 4
c. 2

D3

a. Paragraph 1
b. The main idea is there are many different rooms and many people in his new school.

E

B: False. The custodian works in the hall.

Accept all reasonable answers.

F

Accept all reasonable answers.

G

Answers will vary but may include:
There are many different rooms and many people at my school. The office is on the first floor of the school. The principal works in the office. The library is on the second floor. The librarian works in the library. My classroom is on the first floor. My teacher works in my classroom.

Topic 3 The House
pages 12–14

A

First column: sink
Second column: attic
Third column: basement
Fourth column: kitchen

B

1. basement
2. bedroom
3. kitchen
4. living room

C

Accept all reasonable answers.

D1

a. Paragraph 4: The basement is below the living room and the kitchen.
b. Paragraph 2: The sink is next to the toilet and the bathtub.
c. Paragraph 3: Mrs. Gilman and Tanya are in the kitchen.
d. Paragraph 5: He is leaving early for school.

D2

a. 1
b. 2
c. 4
d. 1

D3

a. Paragraph 1
b. The main idea is <u>there are many rooms and useful things in the Gilmans' house.</u>

E

A: False. Tanya is in <u>the kitchen</u>.
Accept all reasonable answers.

F

Accept all reasonable answers.

G

Answers will vary, but may include:
There are different rooms in my home. In my home, there is a <u>bathroom</u>. It is next to the <u>living room</u>. There is a <u>cupboard</u> in the kitchen. There is a <u>bedroom, too. It is above the basement. There is a big closet in the bedroom.</u>

Topic 4 The Family
pages 17–19

A

Top down: cousins, mother, uncle, grandparents

B

1. mother
2. father
3. Mario
4. Eva

C

A: Mary and <u>Carlos</u> are Libba's grandparents.

D1

a. Paragraph 2: Mary is my grandmother.
b. Paragraph 4: Their children are Cory and Eva.
c. Paragraph 3: I (Libba) am Peter and Mario's sister.
d. Paragraph 2: Carlos is my grandfather.

D2

a. 3
b. 1
c. 4
d. 5

D3

a. Paragraph 1
b. The main idea is <u>the family tree shows how the people in Libba's family are related.</u>

E

B: False. Cory and Mario are <u>cousins</u>.
Accept all reasonable answers.

F

Accept all reasonable answers.

G

Answer will vary, but may include:
This is my family. My name is <u>Clara</u>. My grandfather's name is <u>Enrique</u>. My grandmother's name is <u>Felicia. My mother's name is Carmen. My father's name is Eduardo. My father is Enrique and Felicia's son.</u>

Topic 5 Feelings
pages 22–24

A
Clockwise from bottom: cold, hungry, sick

B
1. hot
2. tired
3. hungry
4. sick

C
B: No, she doesn't. She is <u>cold</u>.

D1
a. Paragraph 2: The girl's father is hungry, so he eats a sandwich.
b. Paragraph 2: The cheerleader is excited about the game.
c. Paragraph 5: Number 79 feels proud.
d. Paragraph 1: Physical feelings are ways our bodies feel.

D2
a. 3
b. 1
c. 3
d. 4

D3
a. Paragraph 1
b. The main idea is <u>people have many kinds of feelings at a football game.</u>

E
A: False. Number 33 is <u>angry</u>.
Accept all reasonable answers.

F
Accept all reasonable answers.

G
Answers will vary, but may include:
On Fridays my classmates have different feelings. In the morning some students feel <u>tired</u>. Before lunch, <u>some students feel hungry.</u> <u>Later, some students feel excited for the weekend.</u>

Topic 6 The City
pages 27–29

A
First column: bus
Third column: hotel

B
1. behind
2. between
3. restaurant
4. the bus

C
A: The <u>mosque</u> is behind the department store.

D1
a. Paragraph 3: A restaurant is on the first floor of the office building.
b. Paragraph 5: There is a temple across the street from the department store.
c. Paragraph 4: There is a mailbox in front of the post office.
d. Paragraph 3: An office building is across the street from the subway.

D2
a. 2
b. 5
c. 2

D3
a. Paragraph 1
b. The main idea is <u>you can use knowledge about a building to describe other places.</u>

E
A: The movie theater is <u>close to</u> the hotel.
B: True. It is <u>close to</u> the hotel.
Accept all reasonable answers.

F
Accept all reasonable answers.

G
Answers will vary, but may include:
There are buildings where I live. There is <u>a post office</u>. It is close to <u>a newsstand</u>. There is <u>a restaurant</u>, too. It is <u>across the street from the police station. The movie theater is behind the police station.</u>

Topic 7 The Suburbs
pages 32–34

A
First column: pool
Second column: gas
Third column: bicycle

B
1. park
2. gas
3. car
4. basketball

C
A: They are playing in a <u>driveway</u>.

D1
a. Paragraph 1: Some of the houses have green gardens with vegetables and yellow flowers.
b. Paragraph 4: Mr. and Mrs. Hong are taking a long walk around the neighborhood.
c. Paragraph 3: Troy and Brian are playing basketball.
d. Paragraph 4: Mr. Clark is mailing a letter.

D2
a. 3
b. 4
c. 2
d. 1

D3
a. Paragraph 2
b. The main idea is <u>people do many things in this suburb</u>.

E
A: False. He is washing his <u>car</u>.
Accept all reasonable answers.

F
Answers will vary, but may include:
The Williams family lives in the suburbs. They were at the neighborhood swimming <u>pool</u>. Jory stops at a <u>fire hydrant</u>. He is tying his shoe. <u>Mr. Williams waits for him.</u> <u>Ani is riding her new bicycle.</u> Two people are walking in <u>the crosswalk</u>.

Topic 8 The Country
pages 37–39

A
First column: fence, tractor
Second column: inside
Third column: orchard

B
1. coop
2. next to
3. pasture
4. tractor

C
B: They are <u>inside</u> the fence.
A: They are <u>next to</u> each other.

D1
a. Paragraph 1: The Garza family has a farm in the country.
b. Paragraph 2: There are many fields around the house.
c. Paragraph 3: Some chickens are inside the chicken coop.
d. Paragraph 4: Two children are riding inside the wagon.

D2
a. 1
b. 2
c. 1
d. 4

D3
a. Paragraph 1
b. The main idea is <u>the Garza family has a farm in the country</u>.

E
Accept all reasonable answers.

F
Answers will vary, but may include:
This is the Digman family's farm. A horse is <u>inside</u> the fence. The cows are <u>outside</u> the fence. An orchard is next to the <u>bridge</u>. <u>Pam and Dave pick apples in the orchard.</u> <u>A neighbor drives her truck over the bridge. The stream runs under the bridge.</u>

Topic 9 The Hospital
pages 42-44

A
Patient: patient, crutches
Doctor and Nurse: thermometer

B
1. patient
2. doctor OR nurse
3. patient
4. thermometer

C
A: The patient lies on a <u>stretcher</u> OR <u>bed</u>.

D1
a. Paragraph 2: A doctor and a patient are in an examination room.
b. Paragraph 4: The baby's parents are waiting to take the baby home tomorrow.
c. Paragraph 5: Paramedics use ambulances to bring people to hospitals.
d. Paragraph 3: One large hospital room has three patients in it.

D2
a. 2
b. 3
c. 3
d. 4

D3
a. Paragraph 1
b. The main idea is <u>people go to the hospital when they are hurt or sick.</u>

E
A: <u>True</u>. A patient is lying in the bed.
Accept all reasonable answers.

F
Answers will vary, but may include:
Tonight is a busy night at the hospital. In one room, a <u>patient</u> tells the <u>nurse</u> how she feels. The nurse is using a <u>stethoscope</u>. The doctor <u>is writing about the patient.</u> <u>Another patient has a hurt ankle. The paramedic is putting a blanket on the patient.</u>

Topic 10 People at Work
pages 47-49

A
First column: mail carrier, computer programmer
Second column: hair

B
1. carpenter
2. mail carrier
3. computer operator
4. hairdresser

C
A: A mail carrier <u>delivers mail</u>.

D1
a. Paragraph 2: An electrician connects wires and switches.
b. Paragraph 4: A writer writes a book.
c. Paragraph 5: The pharmacist puts medicine in bottles.
d. Paragraph 3: One firefighter cleans the fire truck.

D2
a. 3
b. 4
c. 5
d. 2

D3
a. Paragraph 1
b. The main idea is <u>people do many different kinds of work.</u>

E
B: False. The police officer works <u>outside</u>.
A: <u>True.</u> The writer works in an office building.
Accept all reasonable answers.

F
Answers will vary, but may include:
Four people are working in the pharmacy today. The <u>pharmacist</u> is getting some medicine ready. A <u>salesperson</u> is helping a shopper find bandages. A <u>carpenter</u> is<u> building some new shelves.</u> <u>An electrician is fixing an outlet. All of the people are doing their jobs well.</u>

Topic 11 The United States and U.S. Territories
pages 52-54

A

First column: Arizona, New York
Second column: South

B

1. East
2. Arizona
3. South
4. New York

C

B: Indiana is south of <u>Michigan.</u>
A: <u>Nevada</u> is west of Utah.

D1

a. Paragraph 1: There are 50 states in the United States.
b. Paragraph 3: Vermont is in the Northeast.
c. Paragraph 3: Rhode Island is the smallest state in the U.S.
d. Paragraph 2: Alaska is far north of the other states.

D2

a. 2
b. 5
c. 3
d. 1

D3

a. Paragraph 1
b. The main idea is <u>the U.S. is a large country with many states and territories.</u>

E

B: <u>False</u>. Vermont and Connecticut are <u>small</u> states.
Accept all reasonable answers.

F

Accept all reasonable answers.

G

Answers will vary, but may include
I live in <u>California</u>. It is a <u>state</u>. It is in the <u>west</u> of the U.S. <u>Oregon</u> is the closest state to the north. <u>Mexico is south of California. California is a very large state. Many people live in California.</u>

Topic 12 The Northeast
pages 61-63

A

Clockwise from top: Statue of Liberty, stock market, television

B

1. landmark
2. bonds
3. communication
4. Northeast

C

A: Satellites are used for <u>communication</u>.
A: It is located in the <u>Northeast</u>.

D1

a. Paragraph 3: Newscasters report the news in television studios.
b. Paragraph 2: People in finance work with money.
c. Paragraph 1: There are eleven states in the Northeast.
d. Paragraph 4: The White House is in the District of Columbia.

D2

a. 3
b. 2
c. 4

D3

a. Paragraph 1
b. The main idea is <u>the Northeast is an important region of the country.</u>

E

B: False. A newscaster reports in a <u>studio</u>.
B: The <u>Statue of Liberty</u> is in New York City.
Accept all reasonable answers.

F

Answers will vary, but may include:

It is time for the news. People who report the news work in a <u>studio</u>. A person operates the camera. A <u>newscaster</u> reads the news. <u>People in the newsroom write the news. People can watch the news on television.</u>

Topic 13 The South
pages 66-68

A

First column: crop, sugar
Second column: lumber, furniture

B

1. sugarcane
2. factory
3. lumber
4. furniture

C

B: The farmer harvests the <u>crop of sugarcane</u>.
A: Trucks take the <u>sugar</u> to stores.

D1

a. Paragraph 2: Workers make many foods and goods from raw materials.
b. Paragraph 4: Later, workers put the pieces of wood together.
c. Paragraph 3: First, a farmer grows sugarcane.
d. Paragraph 1: There are twelve states in the South.

D2

a. 3
b. 2
c. 4
d. 1

D3

a. Paragraph 1
b. The main idea is <u>the states in the South manufacture many foods and goods.</u>

E

B: False. There are <u>twelve</u> states in the South.
B: The first step in making <u>furniture</u> is to cut down trees.
Accept all reasonable answers.

F

crop, factory, stores

G

Answers will vary, but may include:
First a farmer grows <u>cotton</u> plants. Next, the farmer harvests the crop. Then, the crop is <u>sent to a factory</u>. Later workers make <u>thread and cloth from the cotton</u>. Workers use some fabric to cover furniture. Some fabric becomes clothes.

Topic 14 The Midwest
pages 71-73

A

First column: wheat
Second column: farmhouse
Third column: plow

B

1. barn
2. farm machine
3. wheat
4. grain

C

B: Farmers use combines to <u>harvest</u> grain.
Accept all reasonable answers.

D1

a. Paragraph 3: Farmers turn the soil with plows.
b. Paragraph 1: Six states are in the Great Plains.
c. Paragraph 3: The grain is used for many foods, like bread.

D2

a. 3
b. 2
c. 1
d. 4

D3

a. Paragraph 1
b. The main idea is <u>agriculture is very important in the Midwest.</u>

E

A: Farmers in the Midwest grow soybeans, <u>wheat</u>, and corn.
A: <u>False</u>. They have <u>flat land and low hills</u>.
Accept all reasonable answers.

F

Accept all reasonable answers.

G

Answers will vary, but may include:
I live in <u>Illinois</u>. Some farmers in my state grow <u>soybeans</u>. Some of the <u>soybeans</u> are used to make <u>soy flour</u>. Other farmers in my state raise <u>cattle. The cattle make milk. Some of the cattle are used for beef. These are very important products in Illinois.</u>

Topic 15 The Mountain West
pages 76-78

A

First column: minerals
Second column: cowgirls
Third column: Old Faithful

B

1. mine
2. ranch
3. Yellowstone
4. Divide

C

B: You can see <u>open pit</u> mines in the Mountain West.
B: Where can you see cowboys and <u>cowgirls</u>?
A: You can see them working on a <u>ranch</u>.

D1

a. Paragraph 1: They are Idaho, Montana, Wyoming, Utah, and Colorado.
b. Paragraph 3: People use them to make coins and jewelry.
c. Paragraph 5: It shoots hot water and steam high into the air many times a day.
d. Paragraph 3: People dig mines to get the ore.

D2

a. 2
b. 4
c. 2
d. 3

D3

a. Paragraph 1
b. The main idea is <u>the Mountain West has many important natural features that people use.</u>

E

B: False. People dig open pits to find <u>ore.</u>
B: Cowboys and cowgirls work on <u>ranches</u>.
A: True. They work on <u>ranches</u>.
Accept all reasonable answers.

F

Answers will vary, but may include:
Many people come to the Mountain West. Some are cowboys or <u>cowgirls</u>. They work on <u>ranches</u>. People use <u>minerals</u> to make jewelry. <u>Many people visit the Mountain West. You can see Old Faithful at Yellowstone National Park.</u>

Topic 16 The Northwest
pages 81-83

A

First column: sawmill
Second column: boat, nets, fish

B

1. First
2. sawmill
3. nets
4. fish

C

B: They take the fish to a <u>cannery</u>.
A: They cut trees in the <u>forest</u>.

D1

Paragraph 3: First, lumberjacks cut … ; Next, the timber goes … ; Then, the wood … ; Finally, people buy …
Paragraph 4: First, fishermen use … ; Next, some of the fish … ; Then, the fish … ; Next, the cans of fish … ; Finally, people buy …

D2

a. 2
b. 3
c. 2
d. 4

D3

a. Paragraph 1
b. The main idea is <u>logging and fishing are important in the Northwest.</u>

E

A: False. <u>Lumberjacks</u> cut down some of the trees.
Accept all reasonable answers.

F

Answers will vary, but may include:
Gita's family goes to visit the Space Needle in Seattle. First, they drive there. <u>Then</u>, they buy tickets. Then, <u>they go up to the top of the Space Needle. Finally, they get to the top. They can see all of Seattle and Puget Sound.</u>

Topic 17 The Southwest
pages 86-88

A
First column: irrigation, dam
Second column: well
Third column: hydroelectric

B
1. oil
2. canals
3. refinery
4. electricity

C
A: <u>Oil</u> goes through pipelines.

D1
a. Paragraph 4: Hydroelectric plants use water from dams to make electricity.
b. Paragraph 2: Oil and natural gas are deep in the ground.
c. Paragraph 2: People use natural gas to heat their homes.
d. Paragraph 3: Dams make reservoirs by holding water from rivers.

D2
a. 3
b. 2
c. 4

D3
a. Paragraph 1
b. The main idea is <u>natural resources are very important in the Southwest.</u>

E
B: False. People build dams to store <u>water</u>.
A: False. The Southwest is usually <u>hot and dry</u>.
Accept all reasonable answers.

F
Answers will vary, but may include:
People need natural resources. In the Southwest, there is little <u>water</u>. <u>Irrigation canals</u> bring water to farms and cities. <u>People also need oil. Pipelines bring oil to refineries. Refineries make gasoline and other products that people need.</u>

Topic 18 The West Coast and Pacific
pages 91-93

A
First column: laser
Second column: surfing
Third column: movie camera

B
1. entertainment
2. Golden Gate
3. technology
4. tourists

C
B: What do both actresses and <u>actors</u> read?
A: Both actresses and <u>actors</u> read <u>scripts</u>.

D1
a. Paragraph 2: Hollywood, California, is called the filmmaking capital of the U.S.
b. Paragraph 2: Both actors and actresses make movies.
c. Paragraph 3: People work with both lasers and fiber optics.
d. Paragraph 4: Tourism is important in both Hawaii and California.

D2
a. 2
b. 4
c. 5
d. 3

D3
a. Paragraph 1
b. The main idea is <u>technology, tourism, and entertainment are important businesses in the West Coast and Pacific.</u>

E
B: <u>False</u>. A resort is part of the <u>tourism</u> industry.
Accept all reasonable answers.

F
Answers will vary, but may include:
Our class made a movie about famous scientists. One student was the <u>director</u>. She told the actor and <u>actress</u> what to do. Another student operated the movie <u>camera. The set was a chemistry lab. The actor and actress read their scripts. They did a good job!</u>

Topic 19 Canada and Mexico
pages 96-98

A

Canada oval: province
Overlap: money, national border
Mexico oval: states

B

1. national border
2. Mexico
3. capital
4. territories

C

B: A star represents a <u>capital city</u> on both maps.
Accept all reasonable answers.

D1

a. Paragraph 1: These countries are Canada and Mexico.
b. Paragraph 4: Together these lines help people find places on the map.
c. Paragraph 3: A map legend tells what the symbols represent.
d. Paragraph 1: The maps show important information about Canada and Mexico.

D2

a. 4
b. 3
c. 2
d. 3

D3

a. Paragraph 1
b. The main idea is <u>the maps show important information about Canada and Mexico.</u>

E

B: A legend shows <u>what the symbols represent.</u>
A: True. A legend shows <u>what the symbols represent.</u>
Accept all reasonable answers.

F

Answers will vary, but may include:
This is a map of Mexico. There are three symbols on the map's <u>legend</u>. One symbol represents <u>soccer</u> Another symbol <u>represents baseball. The third symbol represents a rodeo. The map has a compass rose. It has lines of latitude and lines of longitude.</u>

Topic 20 Europe, Russia, and the Independent Republics
pages 101-103

A

First column: Sweden
Second column: Latvia
Third column: Greece
Fourth column: Kazakhstan
Fifth column: Luxembourg

B

1. Balkan
2. Central Asian Republics
3. Baltic country
4. Scandinavia

C

3: Macedonia is a <u>Balkan</u> country.
Accept all reasonable answers.

D1

a. Paragraph 1: A continent is a large part of the Earth's land.
b. Paragraph 5: Russia is the largest country in the world.
c. Paragraph 3: Twenty-seven countries in Europe are in the European Union.
d. Paragraph 5: Siberia is a huge area of land in Russia.

D2

a. 2   b. 1   c. 5   d. 4

D3

a. Paragraph 1
b. The main idea is <u>Europe is made of many different countries and regions.</u>

E

A: False. Russia is a country in <u>Eastern Europe</u>.
Accept all reasonable answers.

F

Western Europe: Portugal, Spain, Ireland, Great Britain, Iceland, France, Belgium, Netherlands, Luxembourg, Germany, Switzerland, Austria, Italy, Greece, Denmark, Norway, Sweden, Finland
Central Europe: Germany, Switzerland, Austria, Slovenia, Poland, Czech Republic, Slovakia, Hungary
Eastern Europe: Russia, Latvia, Estonia, Lithuania, Belarus, Ukraine, Moldova, Romania

G

Answers will vary, but may include:
There are many regions and countries in Europe. One country in Western Europe is <u>Spain</u>. Another is <u>Iceland</u>. Two countries in Central Europe are <u>Germany and Austria</u>. Eastern Europe includes <u>Russia, the Baltic countries, Ukraine, Belarus, and Romania.</u>

Topic 21 Asia, Africa, and Australia
pages 106-108

A

First column: Sahara
Second column: Hinduism, Taoism
Third column: Uluru

B

1. Asia
2. Asia
3. Africa
4. Great Barrier

C

B: Buddhism started in Asia.
Accept all reasonable answers.

D1

a. Paragraph 3: Islam started in Saudi Arabia.
b. Paragraph 2: It started in India.
c. Paragraph 5: A famous rock named Uluru is near the center of Australia.
d. Paragraph 4: The Great Pyramid is also in Africa.

D2

a. 4
b. 4
c. 2
d. 2

D3

a. Paragraph 1
b. The main idea is Asia, Africa, and Australia are important for their religions and special places.

E

A: False. The Great Pyramid is in Africa.
Accept all reasonable answers.

F

Answers will vary, but may include:
Africa has many famous landmarks. The Sahara is a large desert in north Africa. It is the largest hot desert in the world. The Victoria Falls are also in Africa. They are some of the largest waterfalls on Earth. The Nile River is the longest river in the world. It is in east Africa. It flows from central Africa to the Mediterranean Sea.

Topic 22 Central and South America and the Caribbean
pages 111-113

A

Second column: Chichén Itzá, Tenochtitlán, Machu Picchu

B

1. 2000 BC
2. Chichén Itzá
3. AD 1532
4. Aztecs

C

B: Machu Picchu was an Inca city.
Accept all reasonable answers.

D1

a. Paragraph 1: Long ago, three important empires formed in Central and South America.
b. Paragraph 5: He (Balboa) was the first European to see the Pacific Ocean.
c. Paragraph 5: In 1532, Pizarro conquered the Inca.
d. Paragraph 2: The Mayans wrote with glyphs.

D2

a. 3
b. 4
c. 5

D3

a. Paragraph 1
b. The main idea is long ago, three empires formed in Central and South America.

E

A: False. A quipu was a set of strings with knots.

F

First column: Francisco Pizarro
Second column: 1532
Third column: Pacific Ocean, Aztecs

G

Answers will vary but may include:
Spanish conquistadors came to Central and South America in the 1500s. They conquered the native people. Vasco Núñez de Balboa was the first European to see the Pacific Ocean. Hernán Cortés conquered the Aztecs. Francisco Pizarro went to South America. He conquered the Inca Empire.